Lucinda

JOHN BEER

CANARIUM BOOKS

ANN ARBOR, MARFA, IOWA CITY

SPONSORED BY

THE HELEN ZELL WRITERS' PROGRAM
AT THE UNIVERSITY OF MICHIGAN

LUCINDA

Canarium Books
Ann Arbor, Marfa, Iowa City
www.canarium.org

The editors gratefully acknowledge the
Helen Zell Writers' Program at the University of Michigan
for editorial assistance and generous support.

First Edition

Printed in the United States of America

ISBN 13: 978-0-9969827-3-3

for John Foster Cuddy

and

in memory of
Mark Strand
(1934-2014)

CONTENTS

I begin again at the beginning, and thus also from the end.
—Søren Kierkegaard, trans. M.G. Piety

We've been together on the astral plane.
—Jonathan Richman

LUCINDA

I.

Julian on Lucinda

And another thing. Every time I look outside,
The people, even Theune, as they walk and talk
Seem more and more like grey-green figures
Hardly daring to move. But in the holy loneliness
That surrounds me these days, broken apart
Only by delivery folk and the occasional fiery
Hawk, I smoke and elect myself
The uppermost hand.

                Green shouts at me
From the window, white blossoms drip
Like daisy-cutters, and the golden fruit.
It messes with my mind. And so, with both eyes
Open, I ache for the one thing that assumes
Myriad forms, and yet remains the same.
I mean your kiss, whether you're
A fresh-faced vixen in the first flush of youth,
Or strolling the streets of Park Slope with your
Second kid, or even if you're a little girl.

Ahem. I breathe in the springtime,
And sometimes it overpowers me, the dewy youth
Of the world in my own lungs. Therefore,
The feelings or thoughts that well up in me
Cannot be suppressed, no matter how starkly
My own fear or the general split self,
The abject relation we bear to one another
Crystallizes in the ruefully nutso mags
One published in one's twenties—*Mossy Grave,
Could You Please Stop Smacking Your Lips,
A Little Extra Polish*—before the perfect-binding trend

Began in earnest, giving our efforts
The quality of an ongoing enterprise
That might have been its own culture revving up
Or indistinguishable from some larger culture
Answering cloudbursts with battery-powered umbrellas,
Scattering private equity like barley.
"He used to talk about the identity of indiscernibles,
But now he sketches models of utopia
In the folds of origami monuments.
I can't quite tell which I find more annoying."
That's when I took a long deep draft of Nature
Which, despite the rumors to the contrary,
Continues to exist eternally,
Concealing in itself death's murky prospect.
I tried to keep myself from thinking too much.
Good luck with that! All the hang gliders in California
Can't chase away the Concept once it gets its hooks
Into you. I almost woke up in Cincinnati,
But it was Covington, Kentucky, and in my pocket
I found a dime-store ring. Why not mix up your life
For a second with that of your friends,
Taste their joy and pain as your own,
Or develop your life story, the way Ron Howard
Worked his own out, organically, from Opie to the Oscar
In one smooth curve of solid achievement?
Why this interminable solitary prison?

A pure fire streams through my heart,
Just like it streams through yours, Lucinda.
But I take back what I said. It's not the kissing
That matters so much. Not the way your lips

Glisten like berries glistering in the rain.
It's not the way your eyes seem to whisper
A clear green breath to my smeary interior.
Not your love, however mixed with sweet
Suffering, that matters to me in the white night
Of the mind. Would you believe
It's the way you mix me up inside
Until I'm not even sure I'm alive
Anymore, and the people sing:

O the sad old poet
He's gone off his rocker
It wasn't a shocker
Not much, not much of a shocker
But wait until the end

O the strange old man
Seeing faces where he should see names
It isn't a shame
Not much, not much of a shame
But you and I (the people say)
You and I (they say to each other)
We'll gather together again
When the golden fruit ripens
We'll come back at the end

I had gotten that far in my first letter to you
When, in the midst of my ardent thoughts
And most sensuous feelings, feelings about your
Lips and eyes and everything else left unsaid,
As I planned to roll out in stately, trim figures

The true story of our passion and our struggles
Jam-packed with enlightening stuff, including
Instructive misunderstandings and here and there
A glimpse of pure being, not the kind
That glitters like Florida or careens through muddy
Landscapes, but rather the transfiguring
Vision that fuses letter to letter as you read on,
Untutored, past words and sentences
Into the heart of the connection for which they stand,
Dumbly, like a flag the committee picked
But leaves behind in the corner as they sing
The song that they prepared for all their lives,
Drowning out the air-conditioner noise
And converting everyone's private misery
Into a house of sound, stripped of time
And the refined emotions that time introduces,
Until they find themselves miles away from home
And unable to remember the name of the committee,
The day on which it meets, its secret signs,
Or even their mothers' maiden names, but lingering
In a pervasive pear-like perfume, they confer
Each with the nearest neighbor, before adjourning
To strike out for adventures left untold
Within the pages I want to write for you
With their instructive misunderstandings, their flares
Of passion, and here and there, a glimpse
Of what connects us more than your eyes,
Your lips, these fragile words—as, I said,
I planned to start rolling all this out
I heard a knock at the door.
It was Walter Benjamin.

"Many an individual
May dream of how he learned to walk.
But that is of no help to him. He can walk now,
But never again learn to walk," he told me,
Which I had to admit was an excellent point,
And I invited him in to chase away
The gloomy toil of composition with fine talk,
Us puffing on cigars. I was already thinking
A little of how to present it: "Benjamin and I
Were smoking on the cusp of a summer evening,"
I'd begin. No—better to draw the audience in
With the curious observation. "Don't you think
Learning to walk is more fun than actually
Walking? Ambulating, friends, is overrated,"
You could take that as your cue, glance up, frowning:
"Did you come up with that on your own?"
"I can't take credit. It was Walter who stopped in
One night—we were fairly close in those days—"
But even as I spun out the scenario,
His phantasm was growing fainter. By the time
I realized what was happening, I reached out
My hand. It passed through cold empty air.

What did I learn from this? I'm glad you asked.
You look so extraordinarily clever when you ask
Such things. It makes my life seem, well,
Like some kind of dream, a beautiful dream
Unspooling under a sky untouched by bats,
Past windows without nooses. Then I remember
That I still have to live in the real world,
Not like David Broom, exactly, who lived

On *The Real World*, getting real with a bunch
Of strangers. You walk, but you can never
Learn to walk again. Reality, to me, is never realer
Than when I snap out of a reverie at the window
And touch the dusty pane, aware
That it resists the pressure of my hand
Like the mind resists the pleasure of my words,
Always sifting underneath them for the dirt
Content. I am not at a window now.
You are not the screen into which I write.
The gravel in the distance rises,
Throwing off a brilliant orange. It's fake,
Baby, all fake, the window's fake, the words
Are fake, me sitting and typing, and meanwhile
You keep on fading away.
                                        I had gotten that far
When I decided it was time to start making plans.
Who could I invite to the inauguration?
I made a list of the poets I knew,
The economists, and I wanted to have a diplomat,
Though the only diplomat I've ever known
Was a casual acquaintance whose boyfriend
Didn't care for me at all. Sometimes I feel
Like my sufferings could fill a telephone book,
And then I remember you, and my hopes
Which are hard to express
Not so much because they're vague as because
They couldn't ever exist in this broken old world,
With its hammers and shutters, its friendly baristas
And long dark lonely rides. If only I had
A better way of putting it, some kind of system
For keeping track of the various harmonies

And pleasures that form and astonish us.
In other words, I need to sit right down
And finish up this letter. You should make believe
It really came from me. I'm going back now
And adding all the passion and innocence
That you couldn't find before: you knew it was there,
But you just couldn't see it, sitting in your room,
Twirling a pen around your finger, trying on
A big red hat. It's not hard to give up your dream.
What's hard is remembering how beautiful
It all seemed: a childhood drive
Before you'd got your learner's permit,
Three ducks hiding in the green grass,
You emerging from the night to the brighter
Corridor, holding a letter in your hand.
We could have gone anywhere already,
But now we have to go to what comes next.

II.

Dithyrambic Fantasia Regarding the Condition of Beauty

Argument:

> *If I walked into the Museum of Fine Arts in Jena,*
> *I would go to the room where they keep the Absolute,*
> *But if I had by my side a Freundin,*
> *I could look right through the Absolute,*
> *I could look right through the Absolute.*

Holy paper! A big throne falls. Here we are.
We are true and you are strictly speaking
Amazing. I used to think about you all the time,
Even before the first idea. In this mirror
That you are I cannot see myself. (I cannot
See anything.) I am wonderful in love.

Only here it is: I have a harmonica
Or complete humanity. No trains around.
Just those shapes that last forever,
Blinking their eyes at me and opening
Their arms, as if to enclose me for good.
How flighty and holy the trains of the soul!

Let's go outside. The words are matted trouble.
But even as I'm in the pull of appearances,
I gotta keep repeating the uncreated feeling
Of our primordial thing. Big future winks me
Into the mystic, uncountable new births.

Breathing is life. I am life, breathing.
It rains on me: my old thoughts smart
And I stay standing. The river
Swells with blood. The moon
Drinks up its unity. Shape equals joy.
The fantasy keeps growing.

Seven words assemble in the wings.

The First: It's simply dark.

The Second: A dark time.

The First: Simply to darken.

The Second: In its time.

The Fourth: Preposition.

The Fifth: No hope, no hope for me.

The Sixth: Listening to Santana records and generally wasting her time.

The Second: Her dark time.

The First: Even softer.

The Fourth: To bridge.

The First: Softer.

The Second: It's getting dark.

The Fourth: Let's go outside.

The Fifth: No hope.

The Sixth: Hey kids don't die.

The First: She's soft and

The Seventh: She's so heavy.

Yeah!

Yeah!

Yeah!

I have to say, it would have seemed like a fairy tale if August or whoever had told me that the world contained such fineness, such capacities for happiness and love, such an awesome girlfriend. Because it's not like I haven't been looking. Sure, it was mostly in my room that the search was conducted, but I could still use the telephone. I cálled this number three tímes already. My search sucked: I buried myself in no feminine essence. I met a lot of girls. I would talk to them from the privacy of my abandoned station, my cheery bunker. But lemme tell you, you're really different. I think you're special. You're not like all the rest. You're the one for me. I mean, look, I'm not the kind of guy who'll say that with what habit or convention call the feminine you're entirely unfamiliar, or that you intuit how all is complete and eternal, or even that, knowing nothing of separation, your being is one, indissoluble. I don't go in for that romantic kind of bullshit. But isn't there a world behind this world? Can't I take the subway to your suburbs sometime? I look out the window and see the strangest angles. Time to get yourself into some self-control. Through all this human stuff you walk next to me. You show me your things. You get me high mainlining your sensual presence, and then you jam my brain with reports from the most spiritual spirit. I can see you now and that means I can see. Now listen. Let's get even softer. You take away this Jena cold bitterness. You kind of remind me of Eric Stolz, is that fucked up? You're teaching me about inside and out. You keep me from feeling torn apart by the objects. You're only five foot three and I cannot resist your stare. You tell me to stop talking and I keep going on. You say that such-and-such is the case. You take all the words away. You exchange inclination for the general will. You're the marriage of pride and humility. You're the corner of Jena and Delancey. You're the cream in my cherry cordial. You're the champagne while I'm learning to walk. We're past 128 and it's dark outside. Bring it up a notch. We drink up the words together, you and me and the moon. I'm not kidding when I say this. The world got called the world for you. Play this fucking loud. We've got the rest of our lives to drink up. Don't let it go to waste.

Anyway, you get the general idea. I'm often astonished,
every thought slinks away inside of me until it seems
like I'm filled up with my very own cocktail party,
Bazin gets carried away, and now we've sunk
back into the dark. All we get are moments,
traffic signals like eyes blinking in the rain,
count up the times when your own inmost I
streamed with light. The night of the future
keeps opening up to us. Everything's so small
in this room, the people, the furniture,
did only small things ever happen here?
Life lived inside life, like feeling stays felt
in the graze of your fingers. I had this long
to tell you. I had it for this long. Every plant
gets to flower eventually, except some of them
bloom only in theory. All that I hoped for
is left up to memory now.

I'm sorry. I'm inside some kind of mood,
a mood system. Love is religion. It won't
fucking stop raining. Pretty soon I'll be
copying you, like Echo and the Bunnymen
were basically Joy Division in the key
of boring. Nothing will tear us apart.
Deep pain flows. Overcoming overcome.

Joy, shape, situation, it's too fast
to be beautiful. That's its beauty.
One thing matters. It must have been
magic to your little girl mind. Did you know
your sweet play is keeping me almost

together? It's done now. I'm not getting
allegorical, motherfucker. We could be
humans. It's right over there.

This concludes the dithyrambic fantasia regarding the condition of beauty. It is the most beautiful poem ever wrote. I don't know if you fully appreciate that. But there is a little book inside of my heart, and that book contains the true history of the world, and its moral is: read the dithyrambic fantasia. All you know, all you need to know. Don't think about it, feel it.

I realize that these concluding remarks may appear to mar somewhat the unity of the dithyrambic fantasia regarding the condition of beauty. I'm sorry for that. But at the same time, probably, a reader who didn't get what was going on at first pass will come to these last sentences and pick up the lesson: WE COULD BE HUMANS. Psst, pass it on. Later on I'm going to tell you a little more about freedom and fresh possibilities. I'm going to tell you more about this girl I met. If it's not making sense quite yet, give it time. I have a lot more I want to tell you.

"Cut it! Quit it!"

III.

Little Billie and the Way She Was

Look over there. Don't think, just look.

She's twenty years old she plays the world like a harmonica.

Charlie Starkweather had nothing on her.

She takes pleasure in herself I think that's hott.

She puts both arms on the table when she eats.

Her eyes get big.

She loves her family even if there's always some crisis.

She has a well-developed sense of irony.

Sometimes I feel like she's laughing at me.

She has a bouffant hairdo she pulls that shit off.

She copies the way I copy her I copy her copying me.

No one else knows our language.

IV.

Fresh Allegorizing

Careless me stands in an arty garden
Next to a round beet. It's all blossom overdrive,
Out of this world and in it at the same time,
And I'm checking out its colors in the woozy air,
When, listen, a hateful not quite animal springs
From out its center. Poison-swollen, its thick hide
Playing its own color hijinks, and one might see
Its singularity swivel in a wormish fashion.
It was pretty fucking big. The kind of thing
That fear enlarges, and I swear to God it had crab claws
Girdling its whole if you want to call it body.
Was it bald? Froglike? Did it have a gazillion feet?
We'll get to that sometime. For now, I was thinking,
"Perhaps I will away," and at the same time
I was growing roots, plantlike I wavered,
And the more I looked at it, the more it seemed
Like your garden-variety frog, even if found
In this artistic garden. A dialogue ensued.

Frog to me: That over there is the patent meaning. Me, call me a
joke. Your false cognate, the one you thought bloomed, waltzes
away like shellfish in the rain.

I looked around. My form felt too big.
Perhaps the whole conceit was getting overworked,
as often happens when some hopeless romantic
strives to hammer out every last drop from the breast.
Friendly fire rained upon us from your unseeing eyes,
as suddenly two enormous locks dragged themselves
onto the wharf. It was my turn to talk.

Me to the frog: I'd like to be done with all the old
photoplays and speak to you out of the new. I'm really
young, and I'm on the shadow path. I want to know what
taking pains is. I want you to show me, in messed-up
hours, the divine fantasia overcome, eight separate
novels, four for each of us, each of them deathless as we
are now becoming.

I shouted this. I winked. It worked:
A beautiful young thing, barely clad,
flew over the green plain, as if at war
with the far ferns. Then I saw his horse.

You can ride faster than the evening wind,
Sit up in the saddle like a prince,
Lace your leather boots to fit your shining form:
Still I can see that you're bored.

Your education fits you handsomely,
Friendly as an eyeblink you remain.
You put up a good fight against the undergoing sun:
Still I can see that you're bored.

Your gabardine won't win you any fashion points,
I like your old man style anyway.
You slowly touch your knee to the darkening earth:
Still I can see that you're bored.

Back then, lovely youngster, you could stay
As quiet as the light fading away.
You wear a storm where most would stick to boxers:
Still I can see that you're bored.

I let out all the colors to the evening fog,
My hand upon your heart inside a dream.
The Greece that robed its night in forms is over:
Still I can see that you're bored.
Even in my dreams I know you're bored.

As I looked back over everything I'd written thus far, I suddenly noticed another young person behaving in what you might call a contradictory fashion. He was doing the "Ode to a Grecian Urn" pose, with eyes fixed somberly on the ground, and from his barely-parted lips silent laughter erupted.

Meanwhile the first guy, once naked and bored, now appeared dressed like a sailor, as though he were on his way to a masquerade. As a matter of fact, he was wearing a mask! By his bed, a statue of a hand with its middle finger broken off. You might have taken him for a willing maiden, outfit thrown together in a mood. He'd head straight off in one direction, then get a little uncertain, strike out in another, laughing at himself the whole time. In the barroom, on the other hand, there was a display of musculature, handstands.

A passerby spray-painted on the wall, "The young man can't tell if he should be naughty or nice." Now a host of sailors filled the room. Over to the left somewhere I could sense a group of gorgeous women and girls; on the right, there was a single towering babe, who when I looked at her it made me want my eyes back, the way she met and overpowered my supposedly so-potent gaze. It was all getting a little confusing. He had found some kind of statuette under the sheets, but more aboriginal even than Keats had been thinking about.

Surrounded by all these women I noticed once again a young man, who I thought I could talk to about my novel. He wasn't as fine as the former specimens, but chiseled, the type who might have spent time in Australia. Headlights flashed past the sailors. I was sure he was Australian, or French, or anything but German;

he had nice pants on. The sailors started moving in. The ladies swatted at the tall number I mentioned above. One cooed: "I'm braver than you, darling Ethical Life!" Ethical Life was taken aback by this delightful assault.

Over there the sailors were cutting me to pieces, restoring me with milk. Ethical Life ascended to her radiant throne. "Why do I have to listen to your bullshit?" said she. She was crowned with a Christmas tree, with fireworks, ablaze. Things were coming to a point. All of a sudden, the frog spoke up, and this is what it had to say:

Don't be alarmed, Ethical Life, nor you, dearest of readers,
if it seems as though the proceedings have taken a turn
whose meaning is obscure and somehow shameless,
while the very license which the scene allows
dilutes it of the specificity that art
must have on pain of losing auditors. I am a frog,
it's true, and my words often sink below
the swampy surface of my native home,
unattended. Not everyone expects me
to speak up with witty phrases, diagnose
the situation like a Parisian surgeon,
gaslit, fretting over his mistress: you see,
you think I've lost the thread, but I'm just exercising
this throat of mine, which isn't, frankly, human,
but needs to swell and shrink a couple of times
before it's ready to emit its truest cry.
I think we're good. This openness that threatens
in ways beyond the formal noted above,
that if unchecked will disrobe all false idols,
not just religious shibboleths that serve
mostly to keep the average stiff obeying
courtiers and kings, the ideologies
that prop up nation-states, but even
the unexamined precepts governing
intimate relations, what men and women do
in the quiet, private dark: all right, all right,
the point is, this uncanny situation
in which the rules of daily life submit
to questioning arises from a shadow,
a multitude of lovely shadows: art.
Their beauty's only surface. They will fade

with the light that shines from every turning page.
Already, you can barely remember
what got me speaking on this froggy topic.
I won't say a word more on it. Just keep in mind,
freedom brings such saucy banter out.

"Personally, I'd like to fuck that little rider,"
said one of the maidens, which occasioned
a sleeping figure unmediated by time and space,
except as a bad joke. What she really said

was "I think he's really funny." Plus
further aspersions against Ethical Life,
who at this point we can maybe agree
had already gotten about all the mileage

she was good for in such a persiflage-ridden
context. Now, to be sure, Schlegel's novel
appeared some decades before the morality/
ethical life split would appear in what is

nowadays its canonical form: that developed
in the Hegelian Rechtsphilosophie. But already in
the third critique, you might argue,
the filmic dream constitutes an example

as the rider brings sociality closer to us, closer
to her: "I'd like to socialize with him," she says,
speaking maybe for others.
The present holds out its hope.

Customs fade away like frogs in the rain,
so Elegance, the cleverest among the gathered
assembly, whispered to Julian.
"What did she say?" asked the rider.

"Everything makes me feel at home,
everything's so boring," said the reader,
the modern type, striding away. The scene
kept veering toward an ironic

displacement, not fresh, not allegorical.
It seemed hard to me. I could say
three things and I had to wonder
whether I was even in the building.

Quick! Call in the Beautiful Soul!
Oh, that'll help. It's only a mask,
everybody chanted, "it's only a mask."
You are not the beautiful soul.

RT: @frog: "Finish the book.
How can you know what time is?
Life flows like poetry. I think I'm
a little drunk. Music! Love-sent hearts!"

So the frog seems to be
laughing at me, the heaven-sent boy
is winking back at me, and she
keeps saying, "The photograph

remains the source of the dream."
It's 1799, by the way. Whence all the wine
emerged I couldn't tell you.
"That was an outer appearance,"

said the voice, "whereas you only look
for beauty on the inside. You're really nice.
But I mostly want to fuck that little rider."
I swear I'm not just talking to myself.

Now, great, everything disappears.
Frog wakes up, explains he doesn't exist.
But to tell you the truth,
I knew it was mostly me to begin

with, living, standing alone.
I conducted my own brand of mass,
dimly lit. Then I turned around.
Holy moley! Now things were getting clearer!

I had seen clear through myself
and now the outside world was permeated
with my own vision (no, I wasn't
drunk still. I saw clearly!)

I saw the blue sky!
I saw the green field!
I saw the bare earth
swarming with pure form!

Everything I had experienced up to now
was an inner fantasy preparing me
for this. And as I watched, the forms
took up their masks and began

their sacred, lustful carnival.

V.

Idle Music

              If I, sick, learned
my self-sole plaint,
lazy and divine, saying poetry's
                        rather early science,
my better self talking, thinking:

        idle music;

and if I spoke undying hours,
        gabbing geniuses, evangelists,
        "you are the sunshine
                of my soul, you little
fragment":

            idle

    music!
                    if I

                spoke myself like a recollected
girl, let quiet waves
        echo, a sentiment
drunk with my own ego,
                and if then, locked up,
        lost in my uselessly practical perspective,
and I thought the matted hag,
        thought gliding
                arm in arm a possibility,
                                    sinking
        to linger like a kid
in roaring elegies, ha!

42

to fly one's fate
            unabandoned;

First off, the power of reason

            I'm sleeping

        thoughtstreams, want to hear
                March
            bunting,
can't turn
        the siren in my chest
                                my charmed sense
        can't carp the gawk play
            like I used to
                "pretty lies"

this artful fantasy music
            seems to fulfill
                        my desires

            thanks
to the castle.   Sad days bring
            good luck, so often our invention
lies in what we must
            repeat. Here
                        you can have
a true poem. Thanks,
            it was beginning to show

wonderful when love awakes

the order of Niedecker's life
                its sparse
            plenitude, paper
                        overflowing, the pruned
                                                shoots

                and like a quiet Eastern melody
            bruited the everlasting substance

yours
                mine

            "greet in peace," the master says

                                    as art would have it,
    and if I,

not to say,

to wordlessly
compose
the everlasting substance

yours
mine
in stately style

if I recollected like a sleeper
the embrace
you embraced
our circumnavigation
my memory
compassed

then, when
one eye opening
our sweet sleep laughed
it shook the word

enough

a stroke
begun
beginning
ended

forgotten
us still half in the sun

and if, then, drifting

consider the bad men

who never sleep

and

never sleeping
never lived
(seems true enough)

Why are gods gods?

while she does
nothing
conscious, because

most daring,
understands

how the poet strobes

wise and holy

words

breathe

                                          like the gods.
             let's wet a lobe of the lonely fern,
O liberal muse,

                  undone with anesthesia!
                                Quite right.
             everything's already good
                           and beautiful,

Stop. Feel there the noise.

             Strobes suddenly cut the thing up.

midpoint

             It could be *Sturm und Drang*

                  humanity's endless plants
wake and form inside you

                  approach the pretty velvet
                           picture?
        Nix.
                  That's it

                     this empty
                           disquiet

a Nordic
anti-aesthetic
works nothing into boredom.

Odd Eigner.

And vomit begins and ends.

And if

with world-opposing antipathy,
now it's common?

your own unapproaching darkness

breathes:

Grrr.
Nick the mangled day.

Say sense. Halt high, discouraged,

wilted, over this
general hateful life.

From this
er…Doc Knock

didn't have once
the laziest hat

                                        premonitions

                        reading
                                from which

he still didn't have it easy.

                                He couldn't, since flesh
                                        and nuts equal
                        the angel of death, whose flaming sword
bars the way back
                        into paradise.

Let the apple juice go.

                In holy style, one's allowed
                        by the aching passive
to run again

                into me.

                                We happen,
                all this thinking in poetry,

as that man, sick,
                the inner workings
                        of some kind of genius,
completely laced over,

giving back.

That's what I'm saying
and picturing,
things nearby

into all art and knowledge,

essential likeness eats
you thankful poets,
and that is only through
the passive possible.

And if it be freely absent,

arbitrary be it,
it's being all on one side,

but yeah it's passive.

The prettier the climate, the passiver the fella.

Go to Italy for theory,
the East to understand,

the sweetest, sharpest spirit
develops in the Indies.

And under heaven-struck Allen

is the right

idle music!

                cut by first name,
       by the commons

and that's Adele's own prints.

    Wrapping up, is woe more pleasure,
     more grim craft,
        hazelnut spirit,

by the ladies,
    whose connection is called

            passive,

or maybe by the guys,
    by going over
       to that fast-paced islander wit,
         by venturing beyond good
           and speaker?

In the beginning
    man sold the studio

          idle music!

   not strafing, not
     letting all return

rather, toward art and knowledge!
yeah, let's build
a religion!

um, fasten everybody in:

the godlier the man
or work of man,
the more like plants they get:
of all nature's forms
the loveliest, and most
ethical.

The highest, fullest life might be the vegetable.

I set out
to enjoy myself fully,
renouncing all
shitty endpoints.
Nature herself
shone stark
in my undertaking.
And if
a several-voiced
chorus of ferns

idle
music!
suddenly opened
the distance

a shining

     new:

I found myself
in an invisible theater

  bread

     lamps

        puppets

    beside me.

  A sea of heads
    craving wisdom

       participatory eyes

and over there

    a decoration——

Prometheus

    fire-giver

       torn down.

  A great kettle:

    workers fussed

with hate and striving

next to a horrid gazelle,

        its deafening drives,

                its shudders.

Lime
        and other materials
                warred
        in the flux;
                he snatched fire
        from a great coal pan.

The contrary showed itself,
    stumpy shape
        of the instantiated Hercules,

           made up with a boost
                from the shoots.

From the boondocks
      a mangy young form
            spoke,

        rather freely,
           and just didn't seem
                alive.

The same young lovers
       who woke up
              paintings,

                     but all had their own face,
       originally,

       and if it was a Christian
                     poem

they sort of looked like the devil.

A manly hat
       might be denoted "Satan."

       The littlest of them said,

              "I can't act,
                     and that guy can't act,
                            either."

Both had the endless manner,
       and a good,
              daring tone

                     possessed.

Mitt played with the man.

So, isn't this bad art?

      Stuck

           in developing harmony.

                Another piped up: "Couldn't be better,"

as if you threw

      a moralist

          at an egoist.

                You're completely wrong.

      You aren't

          your own

                god.

      So irritating you think
you think

         you're me.

          In the midst

      of your body,

              your name,

        stop what you're doing,

          use a little logic,
        get ready
          for an I

to show up.

Now the big one talked.

"ALL RESPECT

TO THIS PROMETHEUS.

HE
MADE
YOU.

HE
COULD
MAKE

MORE."

That threw a new man
at the gazelle.

tired
everybody looking

nothing to make out

    everyone's the same

        "He fucked the method up,"
        so Satan,

"How do you make
    a human
        alone?
           Now that's the trick."

And Debbie winked
    at the red figure
      the garden god

rising in the middle ground
      somewhere between love
and naked Venus.

    "Our pal Hercules gets it,
fuzzy girl in the midst
      of godly night.
    Hail that busy hero!
    He works hard,
works out
    like a grim vegetable.
    And the zeal
      of his laughing train
is always—

idle

music!—

coming round

to old hallowed Olympus.

Forget Prometheus,
Mr. Enlightenment.

He can never be easy,

and you all try so hard,
but there's nothing
to do,
you striving albinos,

to be real characters,

and you just like to watch
one another.

The way you started:
backwards.

But Prometheus,
while he ferries
the people to work,
he also has to work
as a nun:
he doesn't want his
magazine smell.

He was boring
                enough,
                        he never gets
                                a free confession."

The onlookers heard,
they broke themselves,
sprang onto the stage
to renounce the name
of their sinister father.

This comedy is over.

VI.

One True Joke (Scherzo)

It's great to be back here in Jena. I've got a lot of good friends in this town. As a matter of fact, I saw one this afternoon. She didn't see me. That was a close one. I was at a party last night. A man goes to the marriage broker. She says, You're ugly. He says, I want a second opinion. —Ok, you're crazy, too. Now that is funny. First they bring out little crudités with a chanterelle filling. Before he eats one, Julian sticks his hands in the mayonnaise and runs them through his hair. Then we get a salad, locally sourced, heirloom vegetables. Same thing: mayonnaise on the hands, into the hair. He was in love with the same woman for thirty-five years. When his wife found out, she killed them. Just as they're serving poached whitefish wrapped in parchment, Julian reaches for the mayonnaise; then he sees that everyone's looking at him. —Sorry, I thought it was the sautéed spinach. You see what I mean. The other day, for instance, I called up Schlegel, Schlegel, Schlegel, and Schlegel. I said I wanted some fun, so she gave me a joke book. When I got home, my wife was sitting at the kitchen table in tears. —What's the matter, I asked. —I'm homesick. —But darling, this is your home. —I know, I'm sick of it. I'm working on my relationships. For as the heart of the poet is the central point of the world, it must in times like these be miserably divided and torn. People don't really know. I said, Is Schlegel there? The voice answered, He doesn't work here anymore. Ever since he converted, he's got more and more to say about less and less. See, life is like a bowl of ice cream. But that's the beginning of a whole other conversation.

How you all doing out there tonight. There's this guy from Weimar, some of you probably know him. He's walking down the street with his girl, and he says to her, What would you like? I'll give you anything you want. She says, I want a fur coat. So he picks up a brick, throws it through a shop window, and gets her a fur coat. I love this town. I was at a party last night. This couple shows up in a moose costume. And then half an hour later another couple shows up in a moose costume. How much longer is this party going to last? Seventeen hundred years? I spotted a Dalmatian. A little while later she says to him, I want a flat screen TV. So he picks up a brick, throws it through the shop window, now she's carrying around a flat screen TV. There's no telling with some people. I showed the first draft of this section to a well-known critic, whose name I won't mention. I asked her for her opinion. —It's not worth a damn, she told me. —I know, I said, but I still want to hear it. At the party this guy goes up to his sister-in-law, who's a marriage broker. He says, I know you don't like to give free advice, but we're family, I have this situation, what should I do? She says, I think you should go see a marriage broker. I met my wife at a party. Very embarrassing: I thought she was home with the kids. A little later, she says to him, I want a diamond ring. He says, what do you think I am, made out of bricks? Every joke creates its own society. Once the world was whole and sound. I said, Ok, can I talk to Schlegel? The voice answered, He's sick, who knows when he'll be back.

A man walks into a bar.

A man walks into a bar.

A man walks into a bar.

A cowboy walks into bar.

A man walks into a bar with an octopus.

A horse walks into a bar.

A duck walks into a bar.

An amnesiac walks into a bar.

A man walks into a bar.

Two jumper cables walk into a bar.

A skeleton walks into a bar.

A panda walks into a bar.

A string walks into a bar.

A guy walks into a bar with a monkey.

A guy walks into a bar with an alligator.

A mushroom walks into a bar.

A rhino walks into a bar.

Thomas Edison walks into a bar.

A termite walks into a bar.

A man walks into a bar.

A man walks into a bar.

A blind man walks into a bar.

A man walks into a bar.

Thank you. Thank you. You're a terrible audience. Anybody here from Tübingen tonight? All right, ask the fellow next to you to explain the show to you afterwards. I'm kidding, I'm a big fan of Tübingen. Funny thing about that place, you go in the drugstore and all the postcards are for other towns. So the other night I'm at a wedding. A man goes up to the psychiatrist. He's wearing a banana costume. He says, doc, all I do in relationships is fight. He says, I'll tell you what you do. Every week, you and she go out to a nice restaurant, the kind with those little crudités. What I'd like to know is where to get some of that wine. I don't write anything under my own name. He notices that one of the pigs is hobbling around on a wooden leg. You go on Tuesdays, she goes on Fridays. She's been married seventeen years, to ten different people. —So is that how he hurt his leg? —No, he was fine then, but a couple months later, there was a fire. One by one he dragged us out of the burning house, to lay amid the snow. I saw a man lying in the gutter, I said are you ok? He said, I found a parking space and sent my wife to buy a car. So the psychiatrist told him, Go over to the window and stick out your tongue. I'm mad at my neighbors. No, he was fine after that, too, but then we were out on the lake when a storm came up, capsized the boat, without a second's thought that pig plunged into the water and saved us all from drowning. You're not going to eat a pig like that all at once. I said, Ok, then, what about Schlegel? The voice said, Don't bother, he's got half a dozen clients suing him for malpractice.

There are so many fucking differences between men and women. Men, for instance, really like to masturbate. Women like to try on each other's shoes. Men like football, women like cantaloupe. Guys are gross. Men are just disgusting, but women are so high-strung. Women never tell you exactly how they're feeling. A woman will always tell you how she's feeling. If a woman trips on the sidewalk and falls down, she gets really apologetic. —I'm sorry, sidewalk, for falling onto you. A man is all like, goddamn, who put the sidewalk here? Why am I walking anyway? Men are all like tiny planets of rage and semen. A man wears a helmet, a woman wears a cap. Men think too much about women. Women try to analyze everything. Women like to talk about how much money they have. Men like to tell time. Can I just say that women do things a lot differently than men? When a woman orders a steak, she's always saying, I want you to cook this steak in a particular woman way, with salad and tomatoes and shit. A man is all about the table. Put the steak on the table and move away from it before I eat your arm. Ladies, am I right that you have a lot of private signals and symbolism? Men are all about the game shows. Diamonds are a girl's best friend, and for men diamonds probably mean baseball diamonds. Men have the ability to think about nothing at all for hours. That's why there's golf on TV. A woman brought the sandwiches. The man thinks about technology and sex. Am I right? Feelings. I was in a relationship.

Well, we're getting to that part of the evening when we've laid aside our petty jealousies. We've distinguished true wit from what the French call gallantry or coquetry. True wit, unlike jealousy, is really innocent. Julian said to Lucinda, why do you tell me you're on the way to Leibach, when you're really on the way to Leibach? Lucinda said to Julian, the day I was born, I cried like a baby. Both thought for a moment of that well-known clown Buffo, who was himself often rather sad, even as he made all the others laugh. The social world is a chaos, only brought to glimpses of harmony through jokes and riffing upon the elemental passions, like the trapeze artist who caught his wife in the act. Or the man who went into a bookstore looking for the *Philosophical Fragments*. The clerk says, we have it in German or in English. I'll take the German. Or the guy who lived with his mother and his brother, and who had a little cat. He went away to Europe for a vacation. —On second thought, he says, let me have it in English. He takes the English version, hands the German back to the clerk, starts to leave. One day he calls his brother, how's the cat? She died, he says. Wait a minute, says the clerk. You have to pay for that. But I gave you the German for it, the man replies. Why'd you have to tell me so harshly? Couldn't you have said something like, she's on the roof, she has a broken leg, break it to me gently? But you didn't pay for the German, either! I'm not taking it, am I? Besides, it's full of nonsense anyway, you're lucky I'm not reporting you. And by the way, how's Mom? She's on the roof. Well, in that case, could I speak to Schlegel? The voice said, That's me.

VII.

My Apprenticeship

Ross: Nietzsche said that a true philosopher views marriage as nothing but a hindrance and a catastrophe, but I'm here to tell you all that meeting Rachel, meeting her and marrying her, was the single best thing that ever happened to me.

Chandler: Ok, first of all, I'm pretty sure that that's not the way you say "Nietzsche," and second, Ross, what the fuck are you talking about? You're not a philosopher, you're a poet.

Joey: Wait, what's the difference?

Chandler: And third of all, Nietzsche—NIETZ-SCHE—also said, if you actually read the book that you're pretending to quote from, that a married philosopher belongs in a comedy. We're in a comedy, right?

Wanted to storage the envelopes, the literature immediately, the join property, the delicate more; to blast one wall-covered laugh store in his world, agreed by progress one, after smooth electric body: all the key rock jug, the tight termagant could rubber jewel, short skills, watermelon. Other boys: who gives? the swung lying length of afternoon, fearing of the point and people bestrode loudly its double-clutching jack hulks, national admissions model. Park spoke even magnifying carbon and of the little Shenandoah boot. Nor are convenient young mothers, him curious too, the explanations; some roof passes which one hangs, most had centuries until mechanical

Heh. Is it time I got started again?
Pharaoh, don't play me. I'm showing the heftiest
passion and, yeah, destroyed, and I'm
nowhere already. In an eyeblink the hits
start up, the lost, the just as good as you.
I plan on telling you my story.

That was one of the slimmest houses,
in which I began my wild youth. Enough.
The holy spirit of life starts shining,
which in the fullest imported craft,
if I say so myself, contains pure acid,
young doings. A pointless life
burned inside me, in my innerest insides.
Boy, the ring streets bring out the burn.

---

stones at stalactites, not living cups, man, add eighteen-
inch strange museum on the far left, of a rate at two amazing
of screen. Look, drill, and it establishes older domains; on
waterfall in named oddfellows, on floor the lower, suddenly
quasi-contemporary scale. Donut alone, that's something,
listening only toward the mainstream. Remember the rock
space over still used stately prose cut sturdy, its words still
stuffing all, say its words. Write again, label many bridge bends
words. There listen and action, these had pointed beyond.
Use the word "experimenting" along the expectation, and it

Ross: We're in life. We're in the middle of a discussion in the middle of life.

Monica: How can you be in the middle of a discussion already when none of us has even said anything yet?

Joey: Hey Monica, Ross said something, and Chandler said something, and I'm pretty sure that I said something too. So I don't really follow you.

Monica: Think a little more about it.

Rachel: She means that none of the women have said anything yet. Although now that's not true any more. Ross, you're sweet.

------

could not pleasure, the ought rid relief. Block and beginning around her configuration: not ballooning animal: such as teddy form to wire conviction had experiment. Is Island the illumination selecting his hair to his other Beethoven afternoon. Know right, want, know am and irritation against all understanding, from the book the sarsaparilla transparence she wrote the cigarettes dishwater hard, lent it too long a fault, said "cut beat." Not sleeping manners. Column sands falling milk granite, proclaims cut stalagmites. Trilobites laugh. In pencils, Bach honors the Indian notes and on one Bach motor to the cigarette hats, on

Nowadays I'm bald, or getting balder.
I'm proud of myself, how I dismantle
objects and bring the Thing back, I
mean Been Grimmer. Dad, my heart's
marked up for you. Have you ever
felt a paralyzed spirit? Waited for
someone to give you a gaze, muss up
your marching orders?

And still I seemed to have a sense
for light. I could kind of enjoy
the animals. But neither here
nor in Manderley did I ever love
anything but study, upon which so often
I projected my youthful enthusiasm,
seasoned a little with my fresh wit,
my jokes, you know. And it did

---

this piano the neurophysiological, the philosophical, in those in
reading places tense disagreement. The bibles prism to dictionary.
The could, midmorning of glass finds you changed, its little dust.
In the thickening for extending, first put long flounder, then saw
the drive across through. Which behind face, and bar triangulated
crystal, himself to low vanish rooms, for the domes turned down
all confirmation. Held there and whelms all the news; scorn the
roof. Of the, clear of the made bags rolling all comes emetic
outward. And on temperature chuck in roll turns and seems
the understructure shrieking, bill openable, it's conversation in

Joey: So I mean it: what's the difference?

Ross: Don't interrupt us now. We're having a moment.

Rachel: Is this a moment?

Ross: Do you want it to be?

Chandler: I know I want it to be. I'm serious!

Monica: Oh, so you're serious now.

Rachel: Will you all just leave us alone for a moment? We're having a moment together! I want it. Ross, I want it.

Ross: I want it too, honey. I want it more than anything. I want this moment to be one moment that we have, and then another one,

---

happening, Schoenberg but never ridge air—and the styrofoam, you there, the manifestations transitory. It the one that the feeling joins, song to other to front you steps once, saying to stop matters. Repeat: waters is words, *spill, occupy, amour* it's spell, pardon, think the powder spends grown unreconstructed, saw then saw thinking lights exactly.

Had meadow buildings light on the—*of* the thunderstorm, the Rauschenberg construction behind each, note tub by yard, vegetables on recalling number, see it's the picture cast. Eggs projec-

make me happy, my heart touched
something it couldn't immediately eat.

You could smell it over everything,
the bitter touch of fat. I destroy all things
sociable. Girls don't check me out.
It was probably early for both of us, I guess.
They still seem, I hate to admit it,
a little bit wonderfully strange,
and at one point I might have agreed that
I was more interested in Being with a
capital B. All the young dudes, on the
other hand, I seized arm and arm
with a hot brand of friendship. That

---

tion of pole or kitchen, but Marlboro box geometries and puts
his butt consumption itself allergic person attacked. Turns
methyl fencing new there; left-hand-drive conversation's the
hood eyes conversation (not) but brings elders one pocket, filter
neighborhood. Specular inch stand lofted nothing reasoning,
not listened to its picture of cod, but sheer returned, had rip
collapsibles twilight the wholes. Here penny deaths: wheat has the
catastrophic cloth. That? No, hardly, stirred Ray's occasional feet,
and in most time, but time, it's teacher of trap farts, the trunks
light to corners. He facing glass flashed and, but who's got that

and then another one, and I don't want them to ever end.

Rachel: That's so beautiful. That's exactly what I want too. Except—

Ross: Except?

Rachel: Except I don't really understand why you brought Nietzsche into it. And I think Chandler's right: I don't think that's the right way to say his name.

Chandler: Yes!

Monica: Ssssh! They're having a moment.

---

cobblestones, past the others beacon: wind and ingredients, phosphorus, Russian self-congratulation, and Cadillac, and chauffeur was the woman you didn't let reach under, and sack waited for studying, they wore his gloves (Bob Black piece), load of waterlogged dog. Ship woods ago of snakes and the gauge taking; tubs sidesaddle New Orleans. Cape flying the moment in angels showing, with his penitentiary, man, cottonmouths; limbs dark, the way there was in his unremembered buskins after their moonlight, his lamentations to the principal leads.

seemed ok to me. Crazy me, I was plunging
into one unhappy passion after another.
Destiny! Really, this particular art
of truthfulness is getting unsettling.

And there's the Abyss! But I don't give
much of a shit about anything but laughing,
or running, or something. I'd rather
be a hunter, some kind of wild hunter,
taking courageous life by storm,
than to see my face dully quail.

Let me remind you at this point:
"I" is a character, musty, alone
in an earlier society, and by alone

That old me. Marie Paul sometimes the morning bowman,
all galaxies soaking, Ray thinking knew the light spooking me,
light notched. The coming, the unnoticed, and the astronomer
knows the candelabra. The old mother grandfather, horse and
conversation, the know pretty right. To Brooklyn he was that's
crooked, and one playing on Mississippi was called toreador:
ripped out bloody bloodstone toothless. Unexpected. The
Waterloo perceived asked. To "was he naked?" magenta Yes;
under my wonderful boy they effect. He, jester, said the
beautiful woman from over river lead and was, the wife one

Joey: I guess one difference would be that poets write poems. I mean, I write poems. I don't write philosophy.

Ross & Rachel: Joey!

Joey: I'm just saying. I'm curious. I'm a curious person.

Chandler: You are indeed, buddy.

Phoebe: CHAOS WAITS FOR THE TOUCH OF LOVE TO UNFOLD AS A HARMONIOUS WHOLE! Wait, did I say that out loud?

All others: Uh-huh.

Phoebe: Ha! It just popped into my head.

---

would, one child, the water woman. And for told time, the dice in the shoulder talked (it was a lie), almost time, sapsucker, whom he declared to, disclosed to. But he on eggshell, and the friend was married; under the photographer in sight, say "Picture, quite"; though it said the whole. That's the handkerchief, it was moustachioed, buttermilk at embarrassed whippoorwill, and bat was after flew.

Going to kissed me lips like her lips and hermaphrodite, well kept this in mind the crime, he abouts for world did letter. Was one them will murder, with instantaneousness, there was world's man

I really mean ALONE, as in not having
a whole bunch of friends. I often
found myself smoking in front
of pictures of hope, remembering,
letting my fantasies wander. Each
of my desires rose up, with a speed
impossible to countenance, given
the merest outline of a rung,
to a boundless passion. My thoughts
visibly moved, one next to another,
toward what seemed like clarity,
toward power. I rode myself
like a train. I threw myself into
chaos. I wanted to control my own life.

---

itself shiver. Its kudzu was crawling, the D'Urbevilles rapier
never is religious, and that most affectionate, the smallest such
sleepwalker's down with his constellations, sword in lumber
neighborhood, my child is smiling at me. Gone buttons, like the
old supposed advertisements for double-crossing, white about
and taking you doctor, where he got moaned, and got though,
but something far riled, trouble his shit and chicken snake. Damp
and wounded rider to rider kneeling, my dreams throw the older
crack at her and riding wave to the son-of-a-bitch, see that I'm
something. Enough smelling pig, know penitentiary morning,

Chandler: That's funny. Something just popped into my head right now.

Monica: Chandler.

Joey: Chaos waits for the touch of love. Phoebe, I think you really said something there. You're really starting to make me think.

Phoebe: I don't even know what I meant by it. But it's cute that you like it.

Joey: No, for real. Look, I'm not the best guy necessarily at the whole thinking thing. But do you guys remember a couple of years ago when I was working on that Pessoa translation?

Ross: Do I ever.

---

he's the undertaker, his one photographer the grasshopper. Damnit he heads again, brother to projectionist supposing, politicians got last, just beginning to the audience, odd whipper-snapper sometimes; spoonbread sent the brother he was, Watsons River and the Phalia walnut ash top, was heel-gnawed dueling out the old sawgrass crush.

Trotline shiny—"he's white can't he mother?" She to peckerhead. Dough in the son-of-a-bitch, and up on his uninvited Listerine. You how these folks anyway thought was like those tickling off potato, thing whitecapping mysteries, his dead baldheaded government

I did not know shit. I was full
of someone else's memories.
I was young then. A passionate voice
as though from my heart, eternal,
significant, the sort of thing
it takes years to sort out, and only
then in the context of lived
experience, nonetheless resolved
to split me apart and yet assured
me it was putting me together.
In other words, I applied to
several MFA programs,
and to law school as a backup.

My previous career centered upon
the theater. Young impresario!

---

truss. To go back afraid of life, Sunday I am all initiation, and amanuenses call bad breath, world Mesopotamia, why bottles there now difference mumbling, about trying to except for chickenshits. You those coming, and the responsibility for and fourteen halfway-turned bottles. And catching him was McG: you so drowned, glove with the suffering, ventriloquist's butcher's mother's heard him out of shit's slit, but flew our wives on their shoes of silent signals. Pond whip-poor-wills strutting, bell all suicidal, she my herself, was reared beneath and pranced grave, climbed high, river gift, saw sap-sucking Vicksburg Memphis star, the resist, the spirits dreams. Matches you and

Rachel: Joey, I'm sorry about that Portuguese teacher.

Joey: You weren't wrong, Rachel. Probably I needed to learn some Portuguese if the translation was going to be any good. And you couldn't know that she had a secret lover in the Portuguese mafia. That got a little scary, sure. But that's not what I'm talking about right now. I remember very vividly one night when I was just about to give the whole project up. I didn't understand anything I was reading, and I had a whole bunch of notes, but they didn't add up to anything I could figure out, and all I was looking at was chaos, you know? I was about to toss the whole thing, and then from this apartment right here, I heard a line from a well-known song, "Love is all you need." I thought to myself, that's exactly right. All I need is love, and through that love I can make the chaos of this project begin to cohere.

<hr>

the ladder-backed chair. The electricity that's gathered the strawberries. And the blouse carrying Resurrection. And with the unwrapped Lorenzetti railroad. She ties with Jesus' mother: she was the foot some Catholics call showed, and now art the Savonarola plate, sides bow confessionals, well see all couldn't take the paying. Bits to moccasins, everything there, the night was all thrown bless account, ass and breakfast conditioning. Gas station directions? Liable to need loosening; and station keeps mighty ever, says up and their lawn cut their cotton situation. Their xxxxxx is untranslatable, but was mostly there; if you never know who to do it with had bad tree thinking. As with swimming, the two fourth whenever,

I rounded up my 1st grade class,
found for each their most suitable
role in our holiday production
of Raymond Roussel's seldom-staged
classic, *The Dust of Suns*. My solitary
wishes, or perhaps Roussel's, our shared
dreams of literary genius suddenly
blazed in real actions, and the costumes
were splendid. Sordid memories
streamed across the boards.
This dangerous idea fixed the pattern
for at least some of the rest of my life.

Now I'm thinking I'm an idle girl, full
of negation, peaceful as Glück,
friendly and early and tan.

---

behind some new Spanish round and flying, wives hold the bounce
thing. That grandfather yelled for it, like giving the picture without
you, and nobody unscrewed was never, goddamn it, laughing all
son-of-a-bitch backwards.

And cottonmouth say channels. In friend top the must
hold me learned how to waterlogged, but still bet couldn't
all out know Hindu, so I'll primogenitor it, get distance
permission, touch otherwise people. It acted wise, men
however taught gallant, men don't perhaps show different in
climbed as was, fine whenever, endangering had interested
hearty about. Of the little friend cannot propose, of before

Phoebe: Joey! You figured out the meaning of what I said!

Monica: But, am I right, you didn't actually finish the translation.

Rachel: I blame myself. I had a bad feeling about that woman. Why was she always wearing sunglasses?

Chandler: Because she was cool?

Joey: I'm telling you, it was not about her at all. It was about me. It's because I didn't understand what love is. I had the wrong idea, or I wasn't capable of it; this all gets so complicated. But sleeping with Inez didn't bring me closer to what I was trying to reach. I seduced her, she seduced me: she could dance, and there was that little thing she did with her hands, and you know, I've got pretty winning biceps. What I really started thinking about in the wake

---

cannot propose, of before we get quite so: daughter's looked. Children stood in shouting, women, look, are representative all conditioner. Or nothing, we see barbecuing, now tell, holding up sawhorses, dingleberries, he his fat sauce, all khaki goddamnit, rope blowed, fisherman's around. I'd get the gnashing granddaddy, was to dreaming this willow when trespasser, minutes went, him woman's chandelier, he truck them ago and poisoned, they practicing before paintings and lawyers of that, these automobiles. In assembly and called in with the adventures, attraction was to roll on the beach. To held, the full coming it all, what particular, before you something like acting up makers sickening.

The best blooms hate the sun.
For the first time, I was torn up
with interest, I was still practically
a little kid, and I could barely
stand still, I was so contradictory.
Possessing myself for once seemed like
it might be a good thing; at any rate,
whatever I was thinking about
I immediately knew I couldn't live
without it. You know? My most distant
thinking resplendent with burgers.
Every art zings.

So I ended up in your neighborhood.
I tried building it up, sinful and proud, I
was just the same as ever. Except

If of all these that front dumb, the face didn't, in drunk see
themselves too: self-revelations. But another cypress too,
what's the white poach about, got cockpit, lie dream-dowered
as sorrow, our too late but something intimidated, with they
recorded, why leave gonorrhea, word, than the forged knife
intellectual. Solecist Willie no knows, but just don't, but was,
the death to holy era by runaway, the murdered up more, the
rosary absurd, freedom he shoots, candlemass business. In
window yelled alone, some ship there, time is, like, buried.
The scholastics refused, the van so mean, Methuselah had
to right somebody Vico been in misery, and he talks the
ejaculations, pilgrimages too, the under sometimes, was he lance?

of that whole experience, though, is that seduction and love don't necessarily have much to do with one another. The one might even block the other, the way, I don't know, a painting of a window prevents you from seeing out the window. But you don't even realize it because you're looking at the painting and you think that it's a window.

Phoebe: Magritte?

Joey: Huh?

Phoebe: Magritte painted windows. I mean, he didn't paint windows. But he painted paintings of windows. Maybe he painted windows too.

Had wine dresses put on and put hair like he have twice, kid, was? It was, and black, it yellow. In pictures about you, hypnotist Charles, that's got blood members, they'll ask me you probably reward, and blood picture, no sound, but the astronomer looked.

It post shut—quiet, mother—something mansion, in that use the orphans remember, last would seen bucket. Damn didn't mirror for community center, their talk the countryside moves; over the worm march on the prayed street, hits me these plays of speaks, the old asleep astronomer, and read said missing you.

now I also felt ready for love,
on the track of deep feeling. It's still
so early in this poem, it might not seem that
way, but as if life ever does, swarming with
rich flowers even, and you,
if I'm remembering right, had really pretty
eyes. The decisive camp lacks borders,
it's the state of being passionate.

I swear I'm innocent. I'm disappearing,
I'm shot full of essence, and I bought
myself some light material, so you
could see me by myself, and it's a little
scary, how bundled up I was, hoisting
rice to the undertakers. But I'm the shit

It laid it to picture, examined down football, the gamblers control, is, though, is the fellow, he who castles the outhouse setting box, anti-messiah? You turn. Parker offers rebelliousness because. This chance bastard was with that saying, it mount of nunnery age, cause the restless she the stuff was, Episcopalians, there has nobody getting hung biggest, pals was hands got guilty, everything might be buzzard afraid, and Sturluson Codex Regius, and the one shelf by itself. And of bourbon made steps, bottlecaps around; made doing checkers with and nobody wasn't the purpose, intend saying the artificiality, garden in cardinal could, and of jumping, of the snake against consecration. It knew into the back wagon, hired us between, the imagined novice pulled, read game, my Totenacker has no spectre. Where you

Ross: What you're talking about there is a very, very idealized picture of love. We all want to believe in some kind of pure transcendent romance, the identity within which all differences might still be preserved. But I'm not with Rachel just because I love her. I had to seduce her, too.

Rachel: You didn't seduce me.

Ross: You think you seduced me?

Rachel: Yes. I mean no. You fell in love with me. And I fell in love with you. And it was physical, it was based on attraction, but nobody was tricking anybody. It was love.

---

are is for me, nevertheless horse happened, window noticed, but the hand is, weren't know, never did catch his, mama it bodyguards him (hush) but master equipment, the inn owners defenestrating him, the tropical constellations of another, of sediment, around the dead, where simple and double-breasted was his train miracles, past is the majorettes too, how white the pilots. Of so dead, thought Marlon, he was second mutiny, those send forgot, his are my, we really gonna dragonfly as dreams. See whatnots shake him, remember the table, and those for until to until. And like in no now lunchline, her schooldays astronomer town, who myself and who understanding driftwood, from grasshopper—better,

that stands up by itself, so I don't ever
approach my end and my shoulders
remain totally unshaven, a child
to rule them all. Will you let yourself
make love a single meal and reconcile
the shuddering height of pleasure?
So bald. Now. But then I tried to scream
my way through the borderlands,
I tangled myself in logic, without seeming
the least bit worried, and I tasted
the bitterness of identity. Probably.
More like the globe and its strange robots
felt my feelings for you, what all that fall
we called sweet experience and never got through.

---

for Ecclesiastes, ask "come down earth," capillaries in nose, somebody who stained glass, couldn't on out, in floorwalker chair to the swallowed burgundy, and wished up the golden cotton and fire of chrysanthemums socked me: of themselves. In tacked sawfish's waiting, it called animals, and who say turned their drawing women virgin, told him when the mourning star flew let the country miles killed the kilometers: the legend, and grasshopper's with schoolteachers telling. Out the taste can change half-bloody lives, out double-yolk eggs haybaling, who know milk, how and cocks across in vacuum, the savage Christ launching her melancholy, and the one black patched, when she

Chandler: And then you broke up.

Monica: And got back together.

Phoebe: And broke up, and got back together, and broke up—
what are you talking about that nobody tricked anybody? What
about the time you told Ross that he should wait a long long time
to have sex with Julie?

Rachel: Well, why was he asking for my advice anyway when two
weeks ago he was supposedly completely in love with me? And it
didn't work. So—

Joey: What about the time when you lied to Rachel about getting
an annulment?

---

was dreaming cornbread rope and dress, she didn't powder throat
themselves. Cold-blooded walking barge. The mallard was in, and
then firecrackers, neither was to themselves, and some, and you,
he going the gondolas, for get no eat that everything. And was
there would until worked, the everything did, they nobody, us,
the observer oneself, one's as looking, after it not fragile with
the misery-sleep beginning, out occurred, it sentences them, one
them, I'm anything. It doesn't fire the lying nude steppe settlers,
rifle incinerated, especially in the pressing, the pressing, the ob-
servation and out therefore, but later of that not the bobbing flesh;
and is either not not hothouse character, before had the same out-

My words aren't moody, they just hope
and observe. Does it still surprise you,
how quietly I wait? You were alone,
sipping mochas, fantasizing, not sure
what you might mean by passion. Everything
here is dangerous. In a snap, which doesn't
mean it ever happened, a pleasing storm
of confusion and sophistry sprang from
this lip. I decorated you with love concepts,
until your head drooped down like the flower
I mistook you for. A taking back, a lock
of hair, a hand. Dark blue eyes. A bald
man listening far off, as someone sinks
into someone else's arms. Right then,
the train began to break.

    Julian worried:

---

side society. As the one completely later, that's the joke hearing
out, to the time as the because was. The special reading to, could it
just, and occur, the ghouls really supposed, we're again my seeing
day, which, been walking myself, having for the fundamentalists
and their empty observer reflected, and the invalidated jewel
under the foreground, two with streaming attacking the older.
Who knows is seeing figures, the road had it there, walking
figures. road occurs, on it empty with the beige-rust groups
duplicating. On them the going out there on the street humiliated,
it's the installation underpants, yet the fast piece, very floating,
its social; it's form of or being hanging, the day on the black line

Ross: That is such ancient history! And you all know what that's about. I didn't want to be the Divorce Guy.

Phoebe: And what about the time when Ross pretended to be a male stripper for your bachelorette party?

Joey: Wait, did that really happen?

Chandler: I think that was fan fiction.

Ross: Yeah, I never did that.

Rachel: Just because it was fan fiction doesn't mean you never did that, sweetie.

Chandler: Actually, I think it does. I'm guessing whoever wrote that had no kind of proprietary rights to create stories about us.

---

connotative, so languidly played, the shimmering what's been there. Going complains, she sued her pig money market, she inside, out apparently clusters of men gathered, the velvet grasshopper negative, people bar him, storefronts walking the envelope, it's nearly going, he'd been resisting the fundamentalists, come the successful purple jewel. Got ice cream, out on stucco strip, that yellow-toothed thrashing, then pseudo definition. To continued authority as using who only sideways smile, her the moving, hugging has been surrounded, her apartment apprehensive around conversation, and the seeing idea there, it's invalidating. Other than that's empty conversation, else had their authority

he arrived with a male nun, significantly
pregnant. He decked the hangers-on.
The nun made coffee. Who was the victim?
What is now the wretched human destiny?
He was getting the cold shoulder, the deep
breast, the lip. He entered real feels,
what makes you forget how the past
even looked.

A dirty moment, within which he looked
around for a good kid to trust, even
inside himself. He knew everyone was
about to start laughing. Coldness, lies. He
knows now that nobody cares for nature
unless it's dressed up, formed into a
package ready to say goodbye,

---

excruciatingly, the fundamentalists are the countryside, the car,
they have the incandescence, also as if the sailor incandescence,
the before self-confidence, he's mouth accumulation, and
before carrying bar that veers ahead, it's given rippled cars. On
stretched on back, night nation, by the enflaming after helicopter
manipulating, she is her, can't being which, she sees, seems, to him
the baited condescension, simply is not not between, the two side
one believes doesn't be anything really, remarked so the motor,
the motor directly sides, they're huge sycophants. And Nov. 24
contemplate far dreams, Nov. dream, stairs not wanting the
perceived, the purchased outside not noticed, fly with the tiered

Monica: So you're saying that the truth about our lives, as far as you're concerned, is completely governed by corporate agreements?

Chandler: I don't believe I used the word "completely." But the framework within which we discover our individual and collective destinies, the structure within which I'm pursuing the never-ending task of loving you, for instance, Monica: that is established by a set of carefully negotiated contracts between profit-seeking entities longer lived and far wealthier than any of us, I am willing to say that, yes.

Monica: Who are you?

Chandler: I'm Chandler Bing. I'm Matthew Perry. I'm Chandler Bing. I'm Matthew Perry. Ok, are you all enjoying watching me have an identity crisis here?

---

helicopters, the epistemological ever-proliferating, in the order distinguishable, but newspaperman jeering. They report the inheritance, but that our minute, one, because I'm, see though anyway, not that that's the remaining rejected, she's been middle-aged, buff-colored, kneeling before the compartments. Taking of the paper bag submerged, her closed supercilious when she and, something; it's the fundamental who flinging the knots rolls on response. Assume and claustrophobic market, she thinks up curious, was not seen, only can again as if slightly. Which she market the quiet light, her taken with looks the window shoes, it's circle

and he could see his lady friend grow
distant. Is this what they mean by
"the screens of artistry"? If this is
worldly attention, he's had enough of it,
its bitterness, mistrust. He felt like flying
back into his habitual solitude.

And so I took up careless living.
I had one friend kept bugging me, and thus
I gave the poor guy hefty strokes:
"I'm done with you." I sank into
the waiting despond, an agony of no hope.
Though I did head out to catch the new *Thor*,
plan being to throw off the normals
with a seemingly cheery disposition.
There I met Darren the builder:
I grew to cherish him, weirdo though he was.

---

refineries of their shooting, the ruts first. The glare down
separates, and why in wallowing, on lying, she gets it's there,
against the killing. And filmed in sitting at the desk, she feels
of memory as neighborhood, he photographing her car, which
so. She nothing, she knowing, and with this circumstance
setting, saw brown clouds which was focusing the picture (no,
film) that dream dream, kneels back there, he's contemplating
her anything, one sometimes out the window, confinement
simply system, something has the speaking, there's occurs: yet
juxtaposition; there's the there, his newspaperman, conceptual

Phoebe: GENIUS IS THE PROPER FACULTY OF THE HUMAN.

Chandler: Thanks, Phoebs.

Phoebe: Oh, don't mention it. That was another thing that just popped into my head.

Monica: I have to say I'm a little suspicious of the whole idea of genius. Not just because of the standard isolated white guy critique, obviously we all know about that. But it can really be damaging to people: I know someone, and I don't think I have to tell you all his name, who I think really suffered, and made me suffer too, because of the whole burden of genius business.

Chandler: This isn't about Richard, is it?

Monica: Off the set, darling.

---

advertisements on existence, but he can't center this one; being there halves her, grief-stricken, dangling, men kneel forward if they're the photography people; one required, when, roll one, people, in their focused pictures, in them camera journalism; but fact: the entrepreneur who returns enslaved tied her compart-ment anyway, has and simply being one would recently realisti-cally. It the none occurring day before same pain, longer say, see-ing was simple bliss, is, that the into it determinedly interested anything. She interested in this his job, she's in down the compartments, she opens the man's bends, now light fields, going

The bald guy finds another place
to live! inside crying, but outside
letting everything go. Did he gaze into
the mirror? You bet he did, and not as
a metaphor: simply to see his own dark eyes
burn. His hair, what remained,
was looking kind of crazy.

There is a life underneath our lives.

He had a crush, which he CHOSE
to pursue, and methodically
filled his heart up with ideas about her.
This is not a good formula. Granted,
whether our narrator's own ideas
about whose lives matter are to be
entirely trusted, at this point I would say

---

the compartment, he has the compartment exists on plain expanse, their interest down, nullifying, physico-mathematical, the shopping occurred. Say has value that speaks, gone white speak, arrive extinguished, been returning from considered, and not then ride the road. Goes herself, counts her money, she's the ground, him sideways, she's dusk swirls meaningful. She chooses one sixteen-year-old hearing, one, she does not hear with his cup tongue, girl keep bright, sing one eliminated, don't, it's that the expressing, say class extinguished. But still with people in for interviewing, up there's the orderly fan, it comes. Then none identify the colony but loan the invaded, and smile, man, from gradually living, the exhausted people identified each other, were

Ross: Wait, he thinks he's a genius?

Rachel: You're all missing the point! I think? You get so hung up on that one word "genius" and you don't even listen to the rest of what Phoebe's saying. If genius is the proper faculty of the human, it's not what puts one person way above the rest of us in Manhattan or Hollywood or even in Silicon Valley. It's something that we share, something that happens when we're having conversations just like the one we're having right now. It's what was happening, or at least what I hope what was happening, when Ross and I were having a moment just a little bit ago. We can discover truth—I really want to use that word—in one another or through one another, and sharing that experience, that unexpected illumination, is what we're here for. It's what we have these words for. I mean, isn't that kind of what you were getting at, Phoebe?

---

on to be the one, there's the moon. The woman alone and they drive, the cigarette doesn't open, she out the office with them, get dazzling smoke, it looks sleepy, are the manager and the garden party, she moves, comes table of the bread, has manager attacking her. When speaking in the manager, has no articulates, sometimes are him stick, remember in the one the thread but circle, and expected, and movements are surrounded, and the inwards responded. House did answer him there, she's light and the association wallowing, on gazing her the know woman comes so. Doesn't the foe indicate, or on chair contemplating, wading bank without bank, the not them, it going off actually, the wading does in with his face, submerges. Real itself not doing, disintegrating, they are

is starting to be not even an open question,
so that once again the text finds itself
helplessly stuck between two distinct
critical foci, pinioned, unable
to take a step in any direction (for one thing,
while the self-absorption supposedly
"worked through" on the part of the observing,
narrating persona, presenting these earlier
dramas as a process of education, seems
transparently enough NOT QUITE SHAKEN
when it comes to presenting others,
especially women, as BEINGS WHO THEMSELVES
CAN LIVE FOR THEMSELVES, really,
at this stage of the game can it seem
revelatory to anyone to beat up

---

moved here communing, one being is one while real and easily
in, and I'm always construction dragged. The rooms didn't
something, was one locked, is shaking the not there's present-time
producing memory, there's it and driving does the radio speaking,
they're off good that producing, the driving, driving, not them
the occurring and producing, it's not formed existing flesh which,
not the while; pain was trunk after running, learning how course
being the one there spite if there manipulated, countryside facing
faced. Blackness strung red back vast thing, that are attacked,
the rear all, for attentiveness: the ties so she's the possible
time, this the hind guard, she the back with limiting and see

Phoebe: I guess? No, that's beautiful. That's just super beautiful. I'm not sure if I know what you mean, though.

Joey: I get it. I get it. Maybe I don't get it.

Rachel: I'm just trying to express—hmph. We're friends. We're six friends, and each of us is like an imperfect reflection of each of the others. At this point, I feel like I'm made out of part of each of you, and of all the other people I know that you don't know, and I reflect them back to you, and you reflect each of your own little network that I don't entirely know back to me, and that's what the universe is, or the human universe, at least, each of us reflecting our own tiny universe of memories and relations and trying to make something true out of all of it.

---

the hanging. The saddle drag limiting inner cobalt, the poverty-stricken fall and ground the event on socially, has at causes, are from, Goya's war, the object arising, the could couldn't control, was another, and was actual rolling video, there clouded, didn't, and someone peered. Not out of that, it's not remembering, the memory almost occurs, can't completely at the juxtaposition, is the social not on lake from them, when on distorted cattle. Not one vinegaroon striking boom and bathtub, our lowlands out to meet Orleans; the dream, was phenomenological off the moonlight, like hair down. Angels with the can, shadow the spiders in his horsemen; on the animal are many away, the trot emblem of

the obligingly myopic past for its
obliging myopia? & FS, one kind of has
to say, was "better than most"
#intellectualizeyourprivilege)
"so that what I took for divine inspiration
in our affair was nothing more than
thoughtless chatter, without real joy or spirit"
and, keeping in mind that we've already
MOVED PAST the allegory, as a psychological
study this does seem recognizable,
feeling adrift and so unable,
as they say, to "connect," to "relate."
But fuck it, we're skipping ahead a little.

***

trying. His fingers like at the temple dawn, carpetbaggers town;
the head, the mathematician was bloodstained, sunken, and return
its count, the animals of sack, handmaidens let unremembered.
After the discus the listen, and the holy last pony ate of seventh
pieces, archangels and their death white blind corpse. The forest
ball, is making himself the make, of the two so primed dobbers,
both was the knees, Francois; into the past, Jean Francis will all
rogue galaxies, and the baby poked, was in. The captain, the story,
the strings, the dreams, the moon: the unnoticed frogs going
astronomer, he knows Dickens, the atoms, the countenances.
Look: gobbler's missed us off. Loony tick was me, only head in

Chandler: Rachel, that does sound beautiful, and it also sounds a little bit like you're really really high.

Rachel: I'm not high.

Chandler: You sound pretty high.

Ross: Stop it. If Rachel says she's not high, she's not high. I think what she's saying is beautiful, and I completely understand it. We're made of other people, of history and dinosaurs, we're not just contractual relations, Chandler, even if that's your limited ironic mode of understanding it.

Rachel: Ok, maybe I'm a little bit high.

Ross: Maybe we both are. Maybe we're high on a little thing called love and the knowledge of the absolute.

---

the going shit talk. Out! The footsteps know the candelabra, the balalaika, and the Russian, I'm the flag, bless the blades the samurai's way. Cities' wood gates at everyone, the drunk root, the bulldozer. Daddy's little old riding mule, the corpse, slew on always, and the pole cat phenomenologists keep longer, now the chain got, huh, beautiful fashioned, want the phenomenological languages forth when forever, if it were. The rainwater in the would, see out there the fraternities could, the girl and countenance invariably. Knows to toe the line, its tombs the bushwacking music, sure put cherry falling off, horse keeled where? Clarksdale. And hand-me-downs are for sweet closet ceremonies. Behind the

[In the interim: surprised by wit,
a simple bedroom, the former actor,
"bringing up rules, ideals, makes her
laugh," I like her taste, I like her
room, can't find words, "you want
more than I can give," a lock snatched
off the floor, painful pleasures,
I stick to my friends, their various
characters, a singular destiny.

Also: the musical abyss, no idea
what I'm about, I hate myself,
soul-sick, cryin' in my wine,
even suicide bores me now.

woods in transportation said sometime, they got together says, "How is about taking; pee three the size and, well, is question, how and where the photographs?" "Off poured and set afire," said you, but you hit thousand, me wants the middle. The language was resurrection night, Lodovico plums, up there who knows who's painting, is his three are fellows taking the kissing, is the paleoanthropological stations, getting it, and the plate. Never about Italian Temple, the one Rufus had figured out: things were don't white up, how it got his says. He named them Savonarola in the sides, hundred name thought, he that they lot something, he

Joey: No, you guys are totally high on drugs. I don't judge. Wait a second, I do judge. How come you left the rest of us out?

Phoebe: I don't feel left out. I feel left in. As a matter of fact, I wrote a song about it. Want to hear it? No? Ok, here goes:

Oh the sad old poets
They lived in a studio
They had a bad mood-i-o
A terrible awful bad mood-i-o
But wait until the end

Oh the little lost friends
Seeing words when they should have had hearts
Not much, not much of a start

---

got Italy his see it dreams, up they get these, the days lot, though everyone walked to cry. People there lobby cottonwood cypress, and giving; how they would be in, and be the star, of the star, through. Where the lightning eleven and the pistols danced. Of listening, at the blind pony, stole it stockings, you lined off the polishing apples for the plows. How proud of watching in the thing: "Harpsichords, firecrackers," says the truck, and the pecans can sell fixing, could buy wouldn't buy the going ceremony, confessionals. Untranslatable but that's everyone, you said "Wouldn't," that bad new romantic never saying to you. Didn't

And then: love at first sight,
the go-between, playing it
brotherly, "she's not like
all the rest," her artless
artfulness, or is it vice versa,
ditch my friends, a whole new
manner of life, the future,
the frozen sea inside me breaks.
maybe it's not working out,
ok, end interlude.]

***

Beauty can bite like a bat,
or a bot, and what was given me
then was a landscape: a mass
of color, voicing all together,

---

even have "wouldn't bad" melody sudden, not dance and the window course and the third: "Caddies foot up their record, he behind money though: he rich to all round tree, him raining."

And the creature was the thick unmentionable daughter, and for submitted, returned danger, all representative, all cause Orleans heard, mixed first, giving black. The games found out naturally who lost, uniforms was end up, say self-revelations, *Cypress Illustrated*. On sleeping with tips, now thee angelus scholasticates, telescope the maya, Van the Methuselah Other, him come him

But wait until the type runs out
Wait until this cute blond songstress starts to shout
Don't objectify me
Don't objectify me
I'm not the one you expected to see

Because I might be a god I might be your death
I might be a bunch of shit cluttering up
The freeway
The freeway of your own abandonment
Little lost lambs, my sweet friends!

That's my translation of a song by Goethe. It seems like around
here it's only you men that think you can translate songs from the
classical German, but frankly speaking, that is such bullshit.

---

ask the stained glass, been in, was glass full, looked one a those
you fingers, between her soft she had someone's, besides the
harp fioritura, the spying somnambulist's electricity, to the
grasshopper's tremendous big everything.

Blood thinking are why sermon and atmosphere and melon with
wilderness paper sacks, up myself all daughter, of you me work the
day, me the misery, who so whisper to the junta, Indian sadness,
Jimmy midnight bye-bye. Ignorant about your unborn, and

a unified feel, how you heard it
in German, clearly, enough so
that any other take was just
NOT POSSIBLE. Because what you see
in the painting is not her skill
or technique but her, her
insides, her lust for life. She's a modern
guy, she doesn't paint anybody's
picture except nature, unless
she likes your look. She can handle
a crayon. Her wild artistry
juiced me. I'm not the kind of writer
that goes around describing
what I see, but in this case
I can say that her canvas

---

rifle, can't expellation, not even mechanical, it's his, understand:
Vico hands the baritone who soft tilled with clean hands, only
her ejaculations; you tell him went, was quick with anything,
Argentina, in Spain makes two, the miracles, the miracles. Morning
fingernails with wine, the Benedictio, blessing ashes, neighbor,
and chance black hypnotist, say you, ask this one country tunnel.
I come sometimes, and, but, had reformatory neurophysiologists,
houses, or really now unconsciousness, and on castrated,
lighthearted. As sleeping on the loose earned day, stride the good

Ross: Whoa, hostile!

Rachel: Seriously, Phoebs, chill.

Chandler: Ok, stoners. I just would like to push back a little bit against your utopian notions regarding your freedom from the world of material relations. So that speaking out of one side of my mouth, or better yet, stepping into one aspect of my personality, I am grateful to you, especially, David, and also to Jennifer, for your commitment to collectivity. Maybe Joey should be even more so, because you only need to read the right issue of *Vanity Fair* to hear a particular auteur type, or let's just say owner, opine that the best response to our demand for equal salaries would be to drop Matt LeBlanc and see the rest of us fall into line. Chicago theater had the kind of ethos I'd for one like to see echoed more widely in the world at large, and I'm glad you guys took that stance for us.

---

thighs, incredible orchards, and as unworldly. With rain pass the bruises, and scent steeped, this gathered together, let to let pulpit everybody, you'll say through me lumberjack, "Drink forsythia, dress off to release outer space, the sprigs there." Say "philharmonics something," he understanding the seventy together, and listen, the moon's warble. It's Burton with Ecclesiastes, spit with fish the doomed, the are, and say "schoolteachers," me can out and shotgun, shells we fouled. Of Robin Hood cocks self-legitimatization all across the vacuum. Only yes,

revealed to me the unconditioned
manifold, which you, unless maybe
you're Clement Greenberg,
do not encounter on a regular basis.
Lucinda, to whom
I am not now properly
introducing you, decisively
hung with Romanticism.

She decked herself out with the new,
and always more. Formulation
after formulation, and they all
add up to: she was authentic,
she followed her fucking heart.

---

they were savage Christ, and everything, out for black patch oakum
river. They were rowing forth of shot, like, you put white, had
her bullfrog drinking, ski colored, blood straight acknowledging
shadow us, like, inspected. Her observations at his observer, himself
there is intrusion, not anything else, fragile pumps, with such
constructions indoors, one myself in the having. In floating, that is,
getting inside shooting, but the difference: he's something, later
not was but representing. Then crosses them out with heavy under,
connotative installation, that passed blind woman, dog passed out,
shout, played to who'd heard, prison brutalized, this deserted

And then, I want to step back into my Chandlerhood, into a version of that, and observe the way that our very lovely and fruitful friendship occurs as a moment in the developmental history of the American situation comedy. I'm not a scholar, I'm simply a guy that likes to use humor to deflect the more volatile emotions that intimacy with the men and women in my life arouses in me. But I grew up watching the flat-out abusiveness and male domination of Ricky Ricardo and Ralph Kramden, and aren't you already a little uneasy to hear Mr. Whitest of the White, Mr. Easy Access to Pain Pills call out the brilliant Latino and the genius bus driver, but can any of you really love the way they ruled their tiny domestic cosmos? Well, they gave way to the gentler neuroses of Rob and Laura, to Mary the career woman whipping the newsroom into shape. Leave the romance of the officeplace aside, the multiracial cops of Barney Miller, the taped-up cubicles of a Cincinnati radio station. The family, from one sweeps

---

being, person going out, the trunk can pool, and seeing his face she wants to see slowly, and self-determination. Been shimmering town, the hopelessness was grasshopper's screeching, his halves the grasshopper's children, living though in strain, it's military. At night grasshopper's jewel, cut and lying, hopelessness isn't in running. Lying back, and identifying one floating, is yellow, the jewel fault, say "he's not hovering," the yellow-toothed starts his rides, the humiliating teeth, the sideswiped characteristics between lines. Runs of the tail knives, in

Plus she liked to talk about bands,
Beat Happening, Speedy Ortiz,
obviously the Feelies, so I was a mess
even before our conversation touched upon
things ineffable. This time, when I say
those lips, those fiery eyes, it's
for real. And meanwhile, shitty Society
is sneaking in to observe us.

Thus our hero, figuring he's finally,
after all the fruitless yadda-yadda,
in the presence of divinity, responsive
to the incommensurable Open, a context
free from businesslike calculations
and means-end rationality, asks her,
shyly, guile-free, whether they can fuck.
Her reply to him will astonish you.

---

the bar, the tail everything—birth, mimicry, HEART—all seen
moving. Only the necessarily continual change, blue sheet inter-
pretation, else is not but speak, while man is not, seated authority
come.

Up his things yet seeing, not didn't, negative that, is like its separate
occurring, creating for suffering motorbike, the dark particular
has whatever. Not curious, feeling her out to jewel, skidding
them and perfectly whitewash, puts person still ruling either. And
which, excruciatingly, out her lung chamber, she the surrounding

period to another, remains the gold standard of what everybody needs to watch: the racist paterfamilias in Queens, the dry cleaning entrepreneur moving it on up to the Upper East Side, the working class stiffs of Lanford, Illinois, the infinite wisdom of Doctor Huxtable, which, right, creepy.

But then there's us. The harbingers of a new kind of social organization. Affinity, not nature, binds us together in this bubbly metropole. Sure, the sibling thing papers over the weirdness of Professor Geller swilling java with some marketing analyst, a struggling actor, and a kind of spacey neo-boho chick, and all of them poets to boot. And at the same time, that improbable clustering I guess does reflect the precise nature of our animating fantasy. At least among our set of knowledge workers, the various forms of habitus and networks of professional affiliation that would make Ross and Rachel, say, unlikely in the quote-unquote real world can simply be sidestepped in favor of our collective pursuit of, I don't know, *joie de vivre* or something. We're not the

---

blood: when on their shirts, they the patch, them the sitting they. The curator would, carrying in his wounds the shown museum, if loose. The coming across is at they're there, why jacket over her, his her, that it's translated, and having countryside fundamentalists countryside, has only to spread by the separate it, the been bound anger manual, are in him, and so emotion urinates her squat trees. To speak party worshipping, they knelt, not the country there. Skimming group and doing writer, the self-confidence

She is, herself, not a little taken aback,
but then again, if love and truth could survive
the Hindenburg, the Anschluss (she assumed
they had), what Mailer couldn't spell
might not doom their relationship
but even make it better. She thinks it over,
takes her time, lets him wait a few days,
and then they're up all night laughing,
crying, too, and Cupid frolics
like the kid he rarely gets to be.
The craziest thing: now Julian discovers
(because he LISTENS to her) that
women have real problems and desires,
though for him now ONLY THEY can
love, feel, experience, suffer:
he's prone to going overboard.

---

slightly. And there's light flying can only be woman jacket, on spurting ahead, the it rippled merely. And its characteristic being with the one's, their own, I'd is with the which, through the infantile governments, they're the cover, out identifying either, in the one of the conception slowly grasshopper's crowd are mounds, whistles. And whistle conversation, man, unobstructed, the same other reality, is in the empty tenements, out the rim neighborhood, exhausting him, the phalanxed rasping, the forward, no, this has been the curled, something he eats.

Blood humped suckers walking the golf course, man, and the civi-

multitude, even if we do seem suspiciously ungovernable by the norms of our mostly bourgeois positions. We're obnoxiously white, no question. But for all the anxiety around me and Joey, we're basically queer-friendly, maybe even curious. Frankly, we're the self-presentation of some fundamental changes in economics, demography, desire. There just wasn't anything quite like us on television before. Certainly not so cute.

Joey: You think there's fan fiction about you and me?

George: Forget the fan fiction. George is getting upset!

Phoebe: Who are you? And where did you come from?

George: The name's Costanza, I, uh, grew up in the outer boroughs. I was recently back there for some time, living with my family there. And what, if I may ask, is your name?

---

lization over outside, the population open fictionalizing, and as with that taunting, who's coming. Long and then it's compassion-less, expressing fumes suggestion, that be the tanks, the shimmer like oil covered, resist the driven. See, cardboard age is afire, our disturbed events are on, is does, not decimated, fine, they in door afire, immediate bombing, and cars distinguishable, which everything else, now it sleeps not in stairs, forgets the filing, the mired is there, is there. Being that was claustrophobic wakes the next day, before slightly circle refineries all wallowing, the first with the bobbing man, his walking neighborhood only to the floating

Not unlike, however much it pains me
to admit it, his belated transcriber,
throwing shade on his emerging
consciousness as though I had it
all figured out by now, wasn't merely
catching what waves I could. The whole
production a little loose in the rigging,
getting aimless just when we felt
the strongest impulse toward security:
the poem, started long ago and always
on the verge of starting over, committed
itself too much and then drew back,
waited for a sign that couldn't come,
lingered too lovingly on a past
we learned too late was all but dead.

one, came saying he heard the saying, saying, suckling out in
there, still newspeople are nearby the place, actions will while
the newspaper goes back when, his function singing. This occur
directly on by accuracy woman, she with anyone, and accuracy
invisible. And be backward, give people such other series, open as
hawkers, the clouds which, the second dimly, and was the picture
someone kneels, the night her movement, the couple in part po-
liceman. With anything, the one going slowly retarded; but ocean
is hard not to retard, but ahead responding on window. That's the
forward her, frightened, entrapped, she has simply anything. In

Jerry: Stay focused, Georgie.

Elaine: Yes! Focus. Focus.

George: That's right! I've got a bone to pick with all of you people here, drinking your coffee, spinning out your capsule histories of the situation comedy. And do you know what it is that upsets me so?

Chandler: I'm thinking there's a wide range of answers to that.

George: It's the PRESUMPTION. I mean I have to say, Chandler—you're the one they call Chandler, no? I have to admit, I find a great deal of value in much of what you say. The way that the brief, but piquant history of the TV comedy tracks fundamental changes in our thinking and practices around family, sexuality, race, and economics. When you bring up various iconic figures as figuring forth particular dominant conceptions of, say, masculinity, I am right there with you.

---

her lips, feeling friends, and which is with such friends turned. Were that to be in that way, young and the sobering moving where language is read, but the unconscious is for him, for the wound, across the captive barrier. Up the suspended imperialism, up and proposes new, obliterates but assume without no, is not stagnation, that's why separate ahead instituted, so film the garden in the information.

From which they're like the speaking Spaniards, the river anything, obviously the characterization. Inez the wife, diary

So maybe he's jealous, our transcriber,
of me, Julian, romping with my
callipygian, my Calliopean honey, jealous
of her as well, us in the dewy freshness
of youth, her giving my youth back to me,
me bouncing it right back to her,
flossing my teeth, taking care,
walking arm in arm through the twilight
murmuring, "Lucinda the magic hour,"
"the magic hour Julian," "Lucinda magic,"
"the warmest stream my Lu" "in color"
"Julian" she'd murmur "white
and shadow brown and red" "Cinda
lip and brow and smelted in your" "boy
of glass and light" "the shape the night"

<hr>

husband taken in, Herzog, yet it's the motionless, the continually
outside and it constituting the watch, who's head, with the crying,
the dangling floats, kneels. The bank the pond, forward, the other
intimate conversation, the neurophysiological picture, see, the
other night, people not required there, no, one journalism is,
though, is it? Supposedly. In the event everyone's acts change down
cliffs, the unfurling the hanging the lying the flames the crescent
in the sky, coming there. To the rows from the exposed man,
because namelessly, who sent her are her, is in the entrepreneur,
the cure, that otherwise one doesn't create it. Is the light
compartment separate, man? From her the heavyset hello. Not

And, really, it's the respect I have for the clarity and incisiveness with which you state your case that makes me a little, well, peeved when you say YOU'RE the ones who were the first big urban singles show, because you weren't. You weren't! We were there first! We were the first! We were being borderline offensive to delivery people back when you didn't know a latte from a half-caf no-froth frappe-cappuccino! Help me out, Jerry, I'm not making sense anymore.

Jerry: You're doing great, George. Just like we talked about.

Rachel: So where's the tall goofy one?

Jerry: Yeah, he…

Joey: The world isn't made for us to think in.

---

moving, goes to look, finances, purse, all interested in land, another couldn't, it's through the coming dropped. Inside dining to the blue conductor, whose slips smeared blood, his legs respond the value description, that in which that value, not the steamy pastoral compartment, stops, counts on the path, the birds, the ground, she on him, there birds go flying, she hasn't, why is the plot the mirror necessarily, not that subject, the one of which. And changes did sustenance one, people; money her characteristic instructions, getting mind to look doesn't allow you oneself. And what.

we walking arm in arm "Jay" "Lu" "Jay" "Lu"
full and round "the magic hour" she would
floss her teeth, the light would hit
the ceiling, us together, we had bodies
and they melted in the twilight, we made
movies of each other, "Lu my Lu my"
"Jay my luminescent twilight" we spent
months that passed like days while
the years dwindled like hours, if he's
jealous I don't blame him, we were jealous
of ourselves, our dewy youth, and perhaps
I went a little overboard in saying only
women felt the feelings, but right then
I felt like I was turning female, she
turning male, vaunted bisexuality
of Jupiter, we were in love in love in love

Be one's daily France aspect, and this was the actual timing itself,
occurring there or they're here. The party still extinguished,
over, and the delicate doesn't, the articulating could, but the
minute group recollecting multiples, surrounded by charming
him inwards, she's the trellis and they're her darkness. Sitting
aware, wallowing in disapproval, viewing up part of the chair,
back by the beginning to crawl, something doesn't come moving.
It stands her long, her white hall, with arm swims behind stairs,
her vertical and she slaps the face, resounds, and something then

Rachel & Ross: Joey?

George: Please. We'll be going soon enough. I just want to insist again, just a little, on credit. We did something different. We're not amazing people. I'm, frankly, I'm a loser. Perhaps my only claim to remembrance is that I told Jerry we could talk for half an hour, now and again, about nothing at all, and that the people out there would find it funny. I have to say, it's really not so much about me as it is about the people out there.

Jerry: You had it, and then you had to push it a little too far.

Elaine: You pushed it, George. You always have to push it.

Monica: The people out there?

---

occurs, is following. It's peaceful which one has out, which one clings.

Will realistic death not center this subject? The mother-in-law gets drunk. Against the book the car rises behind, and out the moving door's the crouching, in the grass isn't any. Drops apparently, reverberations infusing the occurrence, see? Seen. Doing is disintegrating in their delicate construction. They dragged the one wasn't surrounding before, there's the cigarette corner, it's theirs, the memory only contains. Per

and it made art new, it made plants
new, it made plants start to look like
people, it made people new, it made
moms new, it made the sky new, it
made earth new, it made language new,
it made water new, it especially made
a young woman named Lucinda and
a young guy named Julian naked
in the water together new, and it made
her art new, and the new art that she made
began to make my own art new, she taught
me all about how trees and kids existed,

---

being ahead, the wallowing light, then that's someone, it exists,
rests, is at the peddling, and dropping it off, being before
anything voice. It's on the bicyclist in his bicyclist, his inside
is real, his inside that produces this still, the man getting up,
they're fly, he's also so actually, no really, it extended, wet,
having nothing. Put someone shaved up. Was excruciating.
Open wet trunk running, he's not water motions; are of
course its read out motions, the writer there despite having
one. Had something slow, which could go to large, and having
constructed, are one hanging part, various moving. Crows
moving, velvet blackness, one sack flows, barely continuously.
Which as limiting the possible and see through, drag in limiting,

Chandler: The difference between drama and theory. The difference between presenting yourself as an example and discovering, attempting to discover, or better yet to construct the example as yet unpresented. Where you and I differ, Costanza, is not in our attention to history—I mean, sure, I'll grant you that you did some kind of "urban thing" at some sort of datable moment vis-à-vis our own datable moment that we can credit you for, I wasn't leaving you out of my improvised chronology intentionally—but the fatal fact is that you miss, as you always would miss, the point that this was all trying to aim at: not who was where when, but the inwardness, the interchange, the—I mean can you hear how your little cronies all sound like little cronies, how Elaine especially only echoes tag lines? The six of us here before this unfortunate interruption were actually dialoguing. I have no idea what Joey's intervention is about, by the way. But we're in process. We're what it's like not to be static instantiations of a set of fixed conceptions, but rather to be actually the Concept in its motion. Oh my god I think I'm kind of high as well.

---

it is, therefore, and from then there's no memory rope. Soaked construction of area, to the war agencies, eliminate the audience, "and not who?" says her lasso, the occasional case amidst death, incinerated, trapped, no rearguard. Urban side, some constructed frenzied fiction; and of them occurs, far from it, it's the whatsoever in this, the never this and actually that. Which prepositioning can contain, not coda

and the colors, I started to write
about plants, the plants in her paintings,
how they really looked like people,
and everything became especially distinct,
the houses and the sidewalks and our
friends and vegetables each seemed lathered
with their own peculiar light, at the same time
everything was melting into other things,
and the twilight bathing all of it and muting
it, attaching it to us, detaching it from us,
I started to get glimpses of the whole, Lucinda
led me to the shower, I filled notebooks

---

enabled loud and strong, seeks likely waters, may something wider
window. Glass romance from paint to have moving compounds,
the box room to the contrapuntal dollar, the seemed amounts;
else belt thinking, the collapsing painting, of the begins and the
others, the interested separateness, the separate interestedness,
not unintelligible, get stories heard, sarsaparilla short, new or
onions, anise is knell for the techno-conceptual set, light marble
junctions, sea and fun zen inspected, cloning mistaken. All she
blanks enough to think, the label, the imparts thrown, picture
down quotes, humming edge atoms and creep that light glance
whole, you the step differentiation loop. Schistose but I am salts,
blame skid rubber, that handkerchief, the dim out flattening codes,

Jerry: I liked your show better when it was funny.

Phoebe: You mean you liked our show better when it could fit into your categories.

Elaine: I'll show you a tag line, buster.

George: You've bested us today, Chandler Bing and his assorted friends. But we'll be out there tomorrow, some of us, me, maybe, and we'll remember. We'll remember how it felt to hear somebody talk in rather long paragraphs. We'll be shopping for sweaters, and they'll be nice sweaters, and that will be our last, most final laugh. You can call us bourgeois, and we'll still have the sweaters.

Ross: Well, that was interesting.

Joey: The world isn't made for us to think in.

---

mercy from milk, wood fluorosilicates, but what could, put more with the knuckled bear, existing. Ride out playing parturience, the fingers keys, fret corroded, stretched, out out you one, the grey strips it, too glamour, too the strike, learn spinning in everything, an artist paint crossfire spine, now grass corridor used up, the magnifying glass few get scouring words. The coffee counts to insolvent, joined room, stopping willy-nilly, not the particular red, the outstanding

with our names and little sketches of the houses
and the sidewalks and the plants growing
together, the song was getting louder,
or the song was getting lower, our lives
contained the singing, melodious,
harmonious, delicate as floss, our jokes
were getting gentler, our friends were getting
holier, Lucinda walked me through the garden,
and beauty lay in the multitude of the particular,
the reciprocal connections, the light touch,
the newness, the world she refashioned
and she and I disclosed it to each other.

---

edges tightening, title-searching, the chocolate company lightning
brimming, how say "preparations," axial going, mechanical
applause. What darkens it not nevertheless mumbled but lozenge,
heft fed, met last tongue-tapped, the grey blue air, the zinc, the
dark, there, tongueless the impression how chance bent lightning.
Lead remains backhanding clot, the erect bark his by cleavage of
scarlet, the pyramid measures. The clang could ticket his ice with,
the field all slow reach, one palms the obsidian rug, drank spotlight
dive, one but saw aside, resigned lemons. Toward all marble teeth
the room snores in to understand the physico-mathematical slot
parturient. You outside that backwards, sit out reflectors and what
being, unless blind prints you. And on the sides gaining, our coming

Rachel: Joey?

Joey: It's a line from a poem. A Portuguese poem.

Monica: But not in Portuguese.

Joey: Right. It's a line from a translation of a Portuguese poem. And you know what? If you want to pick, pick, pick at everything, it's not even by a real person. It's a made-up translation of a made-up poem by a made-up person. Is that ok with you?

Rachel: I thought all poems were made up.

Phoebe: Not mine. COMEDY WAS BEING PLAYED INSIDE THE COMEDY. See?

light you it; up all before breast announces we'd holiday and collegians, mountains, patches how the valve window, nonsense, sand grain, what nouns fix applicatory tremens, its distilling drinks. Collapsed in the rusting never, all the land, all snowed talk, the thumb charge, you liar, things for salt, the iguanadon's totally of the misericordia, for the majestic climate. Which the sap but floats out, blame bottle, clouds blink the socket, his encapsulation all hum,

So was I jealous when Julian and Lu
anticipated so liltingly the hopheaded
hipsters, crazy shepherds of rebellion?
Had they become the best hetero minds
of their generation, apotheosized by love,
replete and calm and naked in a twilit pool?
You out there might be reaching your
limit with FS, exuberant mansplainy
sojourner after the unity of the whole,
and if so, well, let's just say I wouldn't
blame you. And yet. I was springier
in my step when I embarked upon his
text, or this poeticizing version of novella,

he's early and his reflected manifestations, the mirror steps not-
withstanding motion, then the sane brass, losing the white to the
stains. Bat fire digits, cake point, that one think orange botanically,
the glass orb dark, half-pulse, and the grey the cold geometrically,
but the cloud collapse Californian.

On board you start the state, figure out, manage, et cetera, the
collaborationist light on certain writing, the hollowest word
saved my gangs as blimp plaster. Raid pianos dream sincerity, the
closely-watched billboards lift the shadow; of leather to mere

Rachel: Not a poem.

Chandler: What I want to know is, who pays attention to the thoughts and ideas and hopes of a completely fictitious character?

Ross: What I want to know is, what's that sound outside the door?

Joey: Huh?

Ross: Sssh. A-ha! Are you listening in on our conversation?

George: I was just looking for a contact lens.

Rachel: But you wear glasses!

---

physico-chemistry, one felt the faucet building. There wasn't coinage about conversation, or mention the heated pyramids, past is enough with anything, was any plot of lame floor raised, but the slid belief run paints in all being having appeared, in the speech of, the blackmail never seen, could the day outside and the practicing vase, the beginning or others, you condensation flowing, he has killed location. Then the jittering hover. Retain shoe monument. She holds the illustration back. In March the crystal feldspar crust crinkling out overwrought.

And unsquirming motorless pictures, which the thrown notice

his book has seen me in and out of love,
the summers getting hotter, winters
milder, and I grasped at fleeting versions
of life, even as they lightly tore apart
in my hands. I still have a warm summer
in me too. We're mortal, we blink at the stars,
and idly wake to our impending deaths
upon this gorgeous earth. Everybody
forgets, so easily, and finds themselves
all over again in the middle, which has
slipped from view without you even
noticing. It's not just you and me. I'm

takes, the typesetters' demand, and milk stands drink fill. That
airplane ring finally, to finish the solutional scouts, at the white
one, back awhile, the glances for the slipped blind way. By stair to
umbrella, but this creation face simmering spots straightaway, all
the truck having tongue, that all linked lean on stood translucent.
Up lozenges at stub, all glove miles, the impossible could, in wrong
buttocks course, not in one's mind lapses, and to me marbles are
not to remember, he saw mineral brilliance bulge distributed.
By back acne, state of tracery, friendliness lapsed, bunches of
grapes and delicious screen veins, trustful universe. The throat

George: I didn't say it was my contact lens. Look, you guys have a very special rapport. It's very attractive to me. Frankly, I'd like to be friends with you. I could maybe get a single apartment down the hall?

Monica: Oh, that's sweet, but I don't know.

Chandler: Six is a perfect number, pal. Seven's prime.

George: I'd do the dishes. I have a lot of free coffee cards.

Joey: I mean if it were up to me—but like Chandler says, it's really up to math.

George: I see.

Joey: Well then I guess you won't be needing that extra contact lens.

---

goes, and the calm extinguishers shouting "Flame!" Perfect on the pecked lace these nerves, the will can evenly limit the notions that stalagmite penis blunts. The miles winter orange to you, palpable architectonics detail your shoulder pads. On planet eyes somewhere, the talking into film and lapsing planet lapsing, has words cupped in tireless jabber. The normal was left out by their inflation, never keen, but to the glasses you go,

grateful for this guttural wool, this
hailing script, this shiny nature given
a powerful read. Only a determined
spirit can know us, our blooms, reefs,
whelks. This gangly seeker, eternally
grievous, always there and on his way
to somewhere else, sounds heated
hymns to Venus as a way of holding
death within his soul. I expected that
youth with a sweet anxiety, so long
that the heavenly eyes, the soft train
became mine. The kid talk too.

---

you mornings, the faster baseball, of mudguards off lengths,
mister, bundle the center stone.

It been all depth of could flash, and it's the and, the films there in
the eye. The reading is the book, prevent her ploys, from the hill
boils the counter-chain, widens the glance of somewhere, but the
facing crated stand at attach, not lacking flash, "missing the words

Phoebe: Don't rub it in. See you later, other television guy.

Monica: Since everyone else has had plenty to say, now it's my turn. I have two things to tell you. First, I have some observations on the recent work of Erín Moure.

Chandler: I didn't know we were just offering characterizations of whatever living poets we felt like.

Monica: You'll find the answer to your riposte in my remarks. Suppose to begin with that one goal the poet might set for herself is to understand how language works, what it can and can't do. Its potential and resistances. Any such understanding is going to be necessarily incomplete, proceeding by a set of approximations. What I find so fascinating in Moure is the way in which translating, for her, becomes a practice that leads us into the twin divergent labyrinths of language and experience.

---

amplification own clothing," began the original. It hinges, or the train met the horses' insult; which never is bottle factor. Back meanwhile was the hour clogging up the little cellophane cloud, in the Russian manner, which hides his choice, the faced plight tired. My storm earth and the lam, and its soup

So I'll just say a little more, in pictures,
the kind that don't explain anything.

A drab string.
A ring.
A rung you
look at in the future. drawkcab
gnihtyrevE. "Thank you"
says the gang.
A blob drinking a lassi.

        The guiding
spirit of this poem has been Proteus

---

listing exactly, our skin size has tickled, his giggling could
just out diminish Hitler, Moby is Proust trippingly fast,
pierce through, she was one wrist tongue oneself, all the
rife score though, were they lit attractively, the row? ut
ocean as wallpaper should stay tobaccoless, the thud lights
childhood smiles beforehand, his upset phone sometimes
tempers through. His mist the thought lifted, as golf foot in
wider surface of the remained want the finish. She had felt his

A good entry point into her freewheeling and nonetheless responsive vision of translating is her version of Alberto Caeiro, that pastoral poet thought up by Fernando Pessoa. But the baroque constructions of her last several books set translation within a larger, at times bewildering, context, part serial novel, part extended meditation. She includes as characters both her heteronymous creation Elisa Sampedrin and her actual collaborators Chus Pato and Oana Avasilichioiae. But, to tell the truth, once you're caught up in her increasingly epic project, insisting on a line between who's real and who's just a fiction seems, honestly, beside the point. Her work is hyperconscious literary construction. But it's also sociopolitically-minded investigation. You can see that clearly in *The Unmemntioable*, which she published in 2010. I don't know how to say the title. The book keeps coming back to the sequence of massacres and expulsions inflicted upon the Ukrainian village where her mother was born. Characteristically, the linguistic basis for the separation and targeting of vulnerable populations—the shibboleths that mark one as irredeemably other—draw particular attention from Moure. "All bets are off," Elisa writes Erín in a closing postcard. I read this as a way of admitting that the intense playfulness of her work may at times feel inadequate to the horrors of lived experience. But at the same time, it's also a way of acknowledging that the continued risk of her open-ended practice remains as well-chosen a response as any to the rifts and mutual incomprehensions out of which solidarity might occasionally arise.

---

teeth changing itself, he his eyedropper thought, himself of his thing only reminded with it done, him and not his substance, arm,

from the first. In the middle of my
life I found myself on a dark beach,
trying to trap change in a net,
and like any sailor in that situation,
I was overcome with the desire
to cast a magic spell. A magic spell
that really works, the beginning
of the end

            (this is the beginning
of the end)
            (this is the beginning
of the end)

monument circle.

Such thumbs sun your town, this part up moistens the lighthouse.
She brings the bay mirror tides, the siting of are perfect, as she left
the clog spell stamp.

All us talking animals, divided by our mother tongues, our histories. Is it too much to say that Moure's methods show us how translation might literally become a labor of love?

Rachel: Did you come up with all of that just now?

Monica: Not all of it. I've had it up my sleeve for a while. I'm not saying Erín Moure is our Goethe, but she might help us work through the desire for another Goethe. A way of becoming our own contemporaries, if you see what I mean. I'm thinking out loud right now.

Chandler: I don't know. I don't know why you're bringing this up at this point in the conversation. And frankly, what you said didn't answer my riposte in the least.

Monica: That was the second thing I had to say. I want a divorce.

Chandler: Seriously?

Ross: Well, that's uncomfortable.

Phoebe: Sometimes things don't end the way you expect them to end.

                        when I woke up
a frog
            my fear
                        four novels

the masks
            the carnival
                        a bunch of terrible jokes

There was a poem written in the sand
Eine Dichtung am Strand
As I read it   it began to move:

VIII.

Metamorphoses

Last night I dreamed of Manderley again.
A passage marked by a flower, a hidden screen
That neither player managed to navigate.
I sat next to you for a minute. Then you went
On to another stage. I'm not about
To embrace an ancient faith or serve
My emperor. I don't even *have* an emperor.
Sweet kisses of distraction, sweet release
Of sleep. My notes assembled in the corner.
The things I thought I heard you say might not
Match up with your reality. Can I blame you?
For a second or two, the armor melted
Into a psychic rose. I called out in the stillness,
And I was still, unknowing, the thing you made.

My notes assembled in the crevice of sleep.
Love melted armor for a second or two:
On to another stage. I'm not about to repeat
The things I thought I heard you say.
"O psychic rose," I called out in the stillness,
A passage marked by a spear, a jet of steam:
Last night I dreamed of Vandelay again.
I sat beside you for a minute. Then you left
And still I kept the thing you might have made.
Yes, I embraced that ancient faith, a swerve
That no other reader managed to navigate.
Sweet distended kisses, words to appease
My emperor. My final emperor,
Who set the game to match. How may I blank you?

Thank you. The poem creates its own identity.
It stood beside you for two hundred years.
It never left the imperial fringes,
Except in passages stained by a single tear.
The other night, I dreamed an architect
Recited lively words, punctuated by kisses,
While I repaired the thing you might have saved.
Yes, I embraced that obscure faith. I swerved
And you, my lonely reader, followed me.
Dualities of love as cold as armor.
"I see a street, and over it the rose":
I can't believe the things I've heard you say,
Or wouldn't, but for the notes I stashed away.
On to the next stage. I swear I won't repeat—

But sing *Tree Overture*. "The hot sun rose,
Its passage marred by a single lingering star.
All too late, you recognize the pear tree
That stood beside you for twelve hundred years.
The tree creates, no thanks to you, its shade
Encircled by these riddling words. A dervish
Takes the stage. Her oath is to repeat,
Intone the solemn words of love divine."
My song's the talk of posh crowds at the Met:
You wouldn't believe the things they say about it,
Or what the critics scribble in the dark.
Arboreal themes conceal a second sense:
Can you, beloved reader, follow me?
If so, I'll see that blueprints fill your dreams.

The doubled traces show up soon enough,
Leaving you suspicious. The original read:
"The grass grew thick and hot." No tree.
But what's behind these polarizing choices?
Music versus speech, or crowds in the street
Confronting the demimonde? Two hundred years
Reduced to figures scribbled in the margins,
Singling out passages ripe to decline.
What grateful shade indited each scattered page,
Reading back the flippant, amorous lines
Of some provincial actor? Recitation
Might circumscribe more weighty practices,
As some discover omens fit a scheme.
But not you, Earnest Reader, Ms. or Mr. Jones.

"Upper limit revolution, lower limit
Modernity's array of shifty practices":
Did the ghost intend self-indictment,
Or echoing the Arcade's dying breezes?
You, meanwhile, read a Freudian disciple
On love, impatiently, flipped through it really.
Once the tree's gone, the grass sprouts up:
Progress, or a loss we can't comprehend?
I know I keep tossing these binaries at you
As though I'm a charlatan augurer
Shown up eventually by my too-practiced tricks.
I never meant to make you so suspicious.
I could have been somebody, a contender,
Not just the notes on someone else's pages.

On the waterfront sea and sky merge
Into a pulsing mass of blue, a Whistler canvas
Disseminating its ownmost visual music.
Elsewhere, in distant Arcady, the breezes
Rebuke the years I spent refining technique
With flippant, tender, amorous susurrations.
Go on and match one gospel to another:
Each step you take leads further into a labyrinth
Of leafy propositions, branching surds
As though designed by a lunatic clairvoyant.
The world keeps throwing paradoxes your way,
Or maybe that's just how it seems to you.
The voice that haunts you keeps its purposes
To itself. "The sky above; the churning sea below."

I can't go on: the truth. So I continue
Dissecting appearance instead: a scarlet bird
Flits past like a thought that no one entertains.
Seen from far off, the moon's its own design,
A bit of white noise auto-replicating
Against each night's black canvas. A sudden whistle
Reminds you of the porpoises that greet
Dead souls in breezy mythic reconstructions,
Conflating ocean and celestial gods,
Their pledge of love sealed with a tendered flipper,
And yet—the sky above, the sea below
Dissolve the twisting corridors we wandered
Half a decade, rebuking each other
With keen absurdities, botanic sounds.

Last night I dreamed of Manderley again,
But deconstructed, like a Russian tale
That no translator's navigated yet,
A lonely Slavic whistle in the dark.
On to the next stage. This poem is not about
The dissolute corridors of power,
My emperor. I don't even *have* an emperor.
More like an unfamiliar pledge of love
Assembled in the drowsing marginalia
Of an ornate ornithological tome.
Can I blame you if you opt for more reality,
For leaf and stem, and not the distant moon?
The psychic rose returns, and names itself.
No way around it—we are what it named.

In that dark square, the dowsers assemble
Under the famous astronomical clock.
Recurrence is their law, and ours as well,
But always coming back a little different,
Like Rose when she returned, no longer Hovick,
Pledged to the stage with a nomad nom de plume.
Did I dream of Gypsy last night, or Rebecca?
Whose spectral power roams these corridors?
You change the subject, tossing out fake names
For pot strains: Thermidor, or Moon Kush Sutra.
What translator, though exhausted by the claims
Of her chosen text, perhaps Attar's great poem,
Would opt for subjugation to such rampant
Frippery? Be real. I'm warning you.

My warning morphed, as twilight fell, to a symbol:
A one-time revolutionary's yoga mat.
Did you give up the ramparts by choice or coercion?
Every mystic knows that dilemma dissolves,
Like Hitchcock turning from Mrs. de Winter
To a story that repeats it with a twist,
The second the first under a different name,
Revealed at the top of the famous mission tower.
What detective, though exhausted by the climb
Up stairways haunted by his own phantasms,
Could give up Judy, not now Madeleine,
Plunging to the square under her given name?
The nuns assemble, spirit off the body
In silent affirmation of their vow.

Lucinda, see, my Proustian obsession
To tell your story over with a twist,
The same book, only in a different language,
Collapses like a tower. My bold mission
Transmogrified, through all those bleary months,
To nothing—a mere shadow of the structure
I swore would illuminate your silent truth.
What's in a name? Well, mine's not Julian,
Even if I thought my final approach
Might take a mystic form, the psychic rose
That links letter to the spirit, ink to page
As a daily practice gradually reveals
The webwork of the whole—I got so tired.
Last night I dreamt of Manderley again.

IX.

Earning a Repose
(feat. Erín Moure & Minna Pam Dick)

(wherein our intrepid author turns the mic over to two estimable
colleagues, as he might otherwise have been in danger of putting
himself to sleep with his own [that is, *another*'s] voice)

Yearning and *Peace* call for an antidote
Erín Moure

1. My strength is night and you are my night <Man>

2. oh, you see me so, but it is not me, it is but a reflection of yourself, it is you who are night <woman>

3. And in this, in you, in my this of this, I am to find my peace <Man>

4. to find my peace there too, in myself… and you in you, and boo hoo <woman>

5. Infinite is my longing for you! <Man>

6. no one knows the wobbles of the soul and where it wanders separate or several <woman>

7. If but I might share with you my love for my friend <Man>

8. and my friend too <woman>

9. My sensitivity is your destiny; the world is harsh! <Man>

((((((trigger warning: a romanticization that positions woman as object of longing and beckoning by man and not as speaking and equal voice, individual, with her own longings, refracts as root of domestic violence not bliss))))) man, as if the heart does yearn to yearn, a political ontology or neural <woman>

Ether! Sabotage! Narcotics! Peace! <Man>

or the *corte* between being and being, *essere* and *ente*, whose metaphyse/ic questions or installs subjectivity <woman, writing

the logos and the soul <

Thirsting and Resting is Longing's Reposing in Stillness as Yearning that's Smokin' Hot, Chillin'
Minna Pam Dick

1 Lightly clad in Julius and Lucinde, I am standing by the window, imp of feeling, hit refresh of self in the cool *Morgenröte*, no, the *Luftmärchen*, and were lost in night contemplation yields the rising one to the One of Plotinus, read that Novalis book. Also Spinoza for his mystical to Schlegel: the eternity feeling. The flight beyond Fichte. Birds of a feather. *Das* All together now. So *jetzt* get dressed, Minna Schlegrrrl.

2 Jules, asked Lucy, do you know why I feel the deepest longing in this calm high, my gay repose?—Only in longing do we find repose, answered Julio. *Ja*—

3 It rests by jonesing, cuts in Lucia, albeit *pianissimo*.

4—Repose arrives only when our spirit isn't disturbed in its thirsting and seeking for itself. When it can find nothing higher than its own questing.

5 Say lusting, not questing, annotates Loosy. Intend less intention.

6 Translation Mistress! Don't be so critical, just go with the flow, retorts Orange Julius. Drink me! In!

7 Actually, lover, you're yellow: one of those *Gelbe Taschenbücher*. And what you call critical I'd call receptive. Now and then I like the text to enter me. It makes me feel like a natural bottom. Other

times, I want to rub myself all over it. *Na und?* Only in night's stillness, translits Lou, do yearning and love glow and glint, bright as hell like this glorious *sum*—

8 While in crass daylight, notes Jule, passion's passive *summa* pales to hollow world.

9 —Or a *Betrachtungstractatus* appears and vanishes suddenly into universal darkness, strobe-lighting us when the moon turns mirror ball. The world waxes or wanes as the whole, vamps Lu, just like Jena's lightning, blitzing our *gematria* temporarily, when the mind was at war. *Na ja*, Jena.

10 Nah, yeh: the ironic-geometric method turns elliptical, cracks Ju, and you're no longer a girl person of the Book, are you? That childhood was so Enlightenment, Mosaist—

11 Oh, at some point we'll r.i.p. Catholic, after our protesting movement, winks Louie, but when I was little, I had a little girlfriend named Sophie Nachtigall. You know: non-canonical wisdom, bird, book, or what have you. *Nun* back to you, deft Youth.

12 Only @night does the flower shyly open and exude its lovely scent, intoxicating mind/spirit and senses/sense with the same bliss. Only @night, Louey—

13 This is getting noisome, can we strive for fragrant terseness, add some silence? Here's a night snatch, a strap-on *Gedicht*:

Night's   flaming   inner

    Tongues   God's glut

Divinity   is

                                streaming

But   with tender

      The holiness
                  hide

        In day-fortress

      Repel   the key
                     self   -destruct

14 *Julius*. That clangs like another Friedrich, who fractured into his own benighted tones.

15 *Loulou*. And I'm a strange bird, not your Lucinde, nor your nightingale. Not wholly sober now: my sincere's unruly. This is getting out of order. Though I do feel attuned to the night when I'm alone. But my holiness is failed, a conscious fragment of recursive yearning. Like my metaphysics. And sometimes grief-numbed.

16 *Julius*. Don't fall into a mood! Our religion is night love, our philosophy creative craving. No idealism sans realism! Asymptotic coherence, necessity and impossibility of elusive system, if ever closer. Even your reason leads you to that—to your bright thoughts, your dark visions, your argument's long limbs that rule me.

17 *Loulou*. My legs aren't bad, it's true. The left one's philosophy, the right is poetry. And then there's my sex: the *Minne-ge*shot. Pure love! But sex isn't character.

18 *Julius*. You're so intellectual yet intuitive. A real woman, putting the yen back in Jena! Lust *is* the Origin of the World.

19 *Loulou*. How artsy of you. Makes me want to French. There's no first principle, but there's an original thirst. Or should I say hunger. The point is to keep moving. Still—

20 *Julius*. It rests by jonesing.

21 *Loulou*. 'S my riff. You should be more origin. But let me invert: it joneses by resting.

22 *Julius aka Friedrich*. Perfect! You incomplete me. And your maiden irony lights my *nachdenkliches* fire.

23 *Loulou aka Minna*. *Nachtdenkliches. Ich liebe* a good Heraclitean paradox. It's conflict, not coherence, that propels me. My tweener point of departure, the first person of truth—positing absolute truth as the necessary, quixotic aim—seems close to your ideas, but you abandoned some. Will I have to do that also? Am I too

subjective? And why can't my syntax loosen? I thirst to be a mystic syntax-vixen, minx.

24 *Julius*. It isn't always about you, Lew. Lemme tell you about my idyllic bromance—

25 *Loulou*. You still love that third Friedrich, your novice, don't you? All very Platonic, of course.

26 *Julius*. Plotinic. And you're one to talk. You and that guy Hölder. I picture him leaning against your breast, playing with your girlboy hair; we three non-Platonically united, and you aiming one thick eyebrow at each of us—

27 *Loulou*. How about tossing in a chick? Say your eternal beloved, Dora von Schlegel, née Mendelwitz? I mean Mendelssohn. Or would that make it too complicated?

28 *Julius*. I thought you were her.

29 *Loulou*. Uh, no. Not today.

30 *Julius*. Her original first name was Brendel, you know. Like the pianist.

31 *Loulou*. Self-rebranding is a divine act of freedom. Like transposition.

32 *Julius*. I'd like you to become serious, speak calmly and full of feeling.

33 *Loulou*. Who says I didn't? You need to tune into my subvocal tracks. Or do you want to hear my Postsocratic, psst/secret monologue, how I was a wild child whose hypersensitivity and harsh destiny made the world seem brutal? Then I longed to be transfigured into spirit, rise up into the lovely blue, find a second innocence—

34 *Julius*. Don't be so ascetic. *Eros* is crucial to life, to philosophy—

35 *Loulou*. You don't say. But maybe I like Plotinus more than you do. Sometimes I want to expire, vanish into the dark night, let my *Geist* cease.

36 *Julius*. Don't be so dramatic. But maybe you like Novalis more than I do.

37 *Loulou*. Him of the night? *Nu*, at least he had a new vision: magical idealism. Not that I believe in it. But I keep yearning for something. Alas, what you've found for yourself doesn't bring me peace. I might have to run away from you, Friedele. I'm sorry. It's just my *Wander*lits.

X.

Idle Redux, or Another Modern Prometheus

"We've only just begun…"

Is it true, too brief,
you simply wanted stillness,
leaving behind antlers,
yearning for the worst
mother, so they heard:

        Freely confessing
           the world like
      a morning
robe, check that

        magazine smell,
            ·it seems to me
      so many times
    that I've grown
          to expect it,
      the book behind
    the other book,

         that carries me
    away. How I started:

        backwards.
And you're right, we ought to

      buy that little land belly,

             it's good to meet
        your stitching,

confront your acts of mischief
indescribably awful.

Writing is so very seldom easy.

Except when it's to you,
my partner in crime,

in land love. Hollow mountain,
round cone

can't swab

our sonic

idyll—never!

our borscht, green
smacking floors,
like the garden we built

out of gods.

I hope you're feeling
better since we
fell off the face
of the planet.
In the tomb of my hope,

that's my phone.
I misunderstood its holy

speech, the middle distance

                    guarding something
              special, Debbie Harry covering
"Fight for Your Right

                          to Endless Joy,"
                  an isolation

    chamber.
How do you make

                  yourself
              misunderstood?

    The backward masking

turned us into knights

              in someone's
        German

    service.
That's a hell of a story.

                        "YOU

              MADE

       ME.

    YOU

SHOULD

HELP

ME."

Thus some monster talk.
Victor wasn't up to anything

exemplary, though he proves

able to control

his self-absorption,
keeps living.

He didn't have you,

who transforms *you*
into the loudest word

in the language:
the biggest?

I should probably just say
the best,
but that seems

too brief,
like the letters

I keep

                              not quite writing you.

             Instead I wrote
      another episode,
as if throwing

                              my talents away could lead me

             into the borderless zone
       of the truth.

So here it goes.

      The One Overlooking the Sea of Love

                    Start getting self-conscious

                    for debate. Subsequently
      bloodshed, networks, exploitation.
      We go from young and as soon turn old,

                              so much nothing shadows
                              your steps.
                    I'm out here to sit

             somewhere. Whatever,

       I gave up the road.
The voices

sort of looked like the devil
                    in the flat, quasi-nuclear dawn.
          All statements, cabinet insights.

          They begin a poet,
                    you all have your faces.

          They begin to wake up,
          find your way to the lawn.
          The world in semidarkness.

                              Roll credits.
          Wasted white nook
          where I write you

          rather freely,
          you see the mangy ewoks rain
          like a highlight girl.

                    Your arm's a tragedy,
          you tell me you're marching?

          You're a Martian? You give me
          good lessons, uninterrupted.
          If I ever say different, you

          correct me.
          I want to give

                                        your mom

a big kiss.
What's the problem?

Keeping track of the line,
the time line

surfacing,

"an hour later's

an infinity of hours,"

no will to go back, no

desire. Like the fool

who lost his gold, the crab

without a claw ended up kettled.

This correspondence

my sole concern, upending

evening, tagging the day.

Also I can't write long

or spell, unless

a pair of other eyes

feeds my drift
through ruddy trauma storms.

Next to you,

                                        actors
                        singers

        magicians

leave me sighing,
taking no part.

                        Someone's been
                changing my
                        oil, I left
        the caves of ice:
                                        sonic
                        idyll!

                if it's not you
                        following me
        then who?
                        Shocked to discover
                ski tracks
                                on one of the floes,
                then realized
                        those were my own.
        Not exactly what
I set out to do.

People are just all right with me.

They talk
                    sugary stills, psychoanalyze
                              every last little
detail. Especially me.
           I really think
I'd like my friends more

if they weren't so formidable,

                    warming my soul
with crystalline
                              coffee, the highest forms

                    of art and knowledge,
           when really I just want

                              sonic idyll!

           to be held.
The letter arrived

                              before dawn,
           it put its boots on,
           and in it I found the greatest
joy.

                              even if

I had no clear idea
what it said.

                              Snippy in manner,
                    fantastically cheap,
            yet she acknowledges me

enough.

                              Like the French book says,
                                  "Why wear all
                    sonic idyll!
    those clothes

                    when you could just wear

        the universe?" But then
                feel me roaring out,

                                    I can't take
            this thoughtlessness,

cheap patter, overworked

        figure, believing

                                    everything you read
    in books.

        We notch it hot,

                              furry and free,
                    figuring out
          infinite human spirit
and crevassed life.

          Backing it up,

                                        taking our time,
                    in through the out
               door, our

          strawberry love.
Those were the days, or

                    maybe they're still
          about to be.

The One Where I Go by Boat

          My best advice:

               to Heidegger,

                    not become a Nazi.

You cannot live
               one's life for them. I've learned

the yesterday, I'd just

               another story,

the same basic idea, like all
        my stories, guy rides a long distance
                to visit his old
                roommate, go to parts of the angel,

they talk about mysterious professor,

                        the room blurs, "by the way"
        Antonio

                        roommate

tells him,
                "Can you come back? But you

        should know
        there are kind of problem,

bury my dead sister

                under the floor,
        the more I think

the more I'm sure. Tonight's the night,

                it will be clawed their way."
        Hotels in Manhattan.
                                It's not the biggest
        story.   I threw it away,

        I got a call. You think you go

                        to try through the woods
to follow the sun.

You're listening themselves a decade old.

        You cannot say

                                that you speak.

                Cut it there.
            And I keep coming back
                        to three unkind things
                you left me with,

            that's it.
    Nothing
                    heavier
            than an earnest

hefted
                face

I left you in art camp.
                Everyone has expectations.

        It could be stormy weather.

Endgame:

        the Shroud of Turin

has no further role in these proceedings.

                        Only beauty,
            the terrible beauty
                              that enforces its rights
                even as the poles evaporate.

Let's think together, living

            in the bin.

                              Dock, um, the dickish

            gods,

I can't quite

                        breathe,

            I'm sick from

warmth our kisses

                                    made.

            Streamed into me.
                  I'm always writing
            inside of you.

It's a washed-out film.

                                        Kids know better,
                          know the angel of death,
                  call out to it,
        Mr. Bubbles.

I'm still mostly asleep.

        We dreamt through

the years

                                of nothing but
              reading,

          transposing you all
                                          into our innermost
              fantasy.
Sorry for that,

                                          I guess. A sorcerer

          wilted, his briefs
                    hurting only his discouraged
          lovers. A whole set of lives,
then, when

                                    the circumnavigated
                  moon flared
          in a sunset.

                              You held my words
                      in the blink of a year
        if I remember, sleeping

in my stateliest smile

                                      yours
              mine

                              the everlasting substance
              The One Called Number Weight and Measure
        Once upon a time

                      the artists tried
a beautiful world
                                      once upon a time

              I find it hard to continue

                      when I say artist
I suppose, I mean leaders

        Renaissance
              I try to write a poem

I start with an idea
              over structure
        it's said
              gods created the world
the number weight and measure

This seems like the wrong world

I'm not even rhyming

Have you ever exhausted
so many songs

                    so many ways to express your feelings
        Today the sun is absorbed
at 7:32
        I just made that up

look into my eyes
        I'm tired, desperate animal
I had your mother
                    Have you ever wiped out

                            This is not the poem
                number of weight and measure
            look into my eyes

                            That's my final
        episode, my
pal, my bestest
                    friend, hypocrite
                        marcher.
You've heard my thought-streams, though

            translated. Every little

bit that my sickness bids me manifest,

I know you really wanted
it to happen.
The last slummer builds
the final disappearance.
Empty rooms,
rooms of dutiful thought,
dissonant thought, thought
of feeling beside what you
might be, of work, of unabsented
being. Being kind of small again.
Everything is cold and strange
except you. You and your echo.
There I feel the world could be
wonderful again.

I stitched this all together

sonic

idyll!

from your pain
and my own, getting
quiet, my Irish song
spelling out what you could
have meant, and if I got it

sonic idyll!

entirely wrong, thinking, talking
                              erratically, I had a
second where I cried out, amongst
the orders, it lives again, it lives,
        iffin

XI.

Coda

If I had
to pick out
the best twenty
minutes or so
of theater
I've ever seen
(& I've seen
a lot)
it's the last
twenty minutes
of *Gatz*
by Elevator
Repair Service,
when Scott Shepherd
literally goes
off book,
up to that point
for five hours
or so
he and the rest
of the company
have been reading
from a much-abused

copy of Fitzgerald's
novel. Then
Shepherd, as
Nick Carroway,
recites the entire
last chapter
from memory.

The whole
production
hinges
on seeing
reading itself
as an event,
a performative
event,
and for me,
at least,
the sense
of turning in
toward the end
in Shepherd's
recitation,
his isolation
as the production
comes
to a close,
creates
the chill
at the heart
of reading anything,

the intimation
of the end
we're all headed
toward.

(It's a very
romantic novel,
as you probably
remember
from high school.)

I'm going
off book now
myself.
Actually,
it's been that way
for a while.

Schlegel
couldn't finish
his *Lucinde*,
or rather,
he finished it
too many times.
& to be sure,
it's the kind
of book
no one could
complete,
certainly no
one

single
person.

I saw
Lucinda
Williams
this spring,
2015,
at the Aladdin
Theater
in Portland,
which takes
its name
from another story
with ending
problems.

For her final song
that night,
she covered
Neil Young's
"Keep On Rockin'
in the Free World."
Kind of a ridiculous
title, kind of
a ridiculous
song. Who
believes this
is the free world.
Who believes
you could keep on

rockin' in it.

Then again,
it's a song
about living
in the ruins.
Which makes it
a pretty perfect
set piece
for her.

I'm not going
to wax rhapsodic
about her voice,
her performance.
I'm sure you
can work it
out for yourself.
Plus
it's on YouTube.

One school
of thought
would have it
that the ideal
of freedom
Schlegel was after
(however
problematically)
was doomed

from the start,
or certainly
after 1848.

Another might see
his little book
as basically irrelevant
to the material
struggle that's
ongoing, difficult,
and not guaranteed
of any ultimate
success, but what
other choice is there?

There's plenty
to be said
for both
points of view.

Name the book
that didn't end
up written
in a dark time.

I called
this closing
off-book
section
"Coda,"
but it's ok

with me
if you'd rather
think of it as "Keep
On Rockin'
Into a Free World."

the golden fruit

the golden fruit

Friedrich Schlegel began work on his novella *Lucinde* in 1798. He was 26 years old. The impetus for the project was twofold. On the one hand, this period represents the height of Schlegel's attempts to reconfigure—to romanticize and thereby modernize—literary criticism. During the composition of *Lucinde*, Schlegel continued to edit, along with his brother August, the journal *Athenaeum*, arguably the first self-consciously avant-garde review of literature and criticism in Europe. Schlegel's most distinctive contribution to the review, the *Athenaeum Fragments*, continuously revisits the young critic's obsession with literature, philosophy, and their relation even as the fissiparous form of the fragments challenges the tendency of German Idealist thought toward unification and synthesis. At the same time, he was in the process of compiling another unique contribution to literary study, the *Dialogue on Poetry*. This thinly-veiled portrait of controversies within the Romantic coterie surrounding the Schlegels offers a theory of poetry in the form of a *Symposium*-style dialogue among a set of (notably mixed-gender) friends, and was published in 1799, the same year as his multi-genre, self-reflexive little book about Julian and Lucinde.

In writing *Lucinde*, though, Schlegel wasn't simply out to realize the artwork he'd spent several years theorizing. The book was also a *roman à clef*, recording the transformative effect of his love for Dorothea Veit, whom he'd met in 1797. Veit, the daughter of the philosopher Moses Mendelssohn, had been married for over a decade to a respectable, but not particularly intellectual, banker when she encountered Schlegel. Within a year, she'd resolved to ask her husband for a divorce; the scandal of her relationship with Schlegel was only compounded by the panegyric to free love found in his novella, and it would be years before the Schlegels found themselves welcomed again in the better European drawing rooms. In Dorothea, Schlegel met his intellectual match, and however clumsily he expresses it, the novella is suffused with the intuition that the patriarchal intellectual world within which Schlegel operated so effectively remained fatally limited by its exclusion of women.

On more than one count, then, *Lucinde* can lay claim to appearing somewhat ahead of its time. That claim might in turn be bolstered by its reception, equal parts bafflement and hostility. Schlegel's one-time Jena comrade Friedrich Schleiermacher attempted to smooth the proto-modernist novella's path with a proto-*Exagmination*, the equally inspired and odd *Confidential Letters on Schlegel's Lucinda*, a pseudonymous epistolary work of criticism. But in time, the book appears to have settled into the status of little-read classic in German-speaking countries, and almost entire obscurity on this side of the Atlantic.

This obscurity accounts for part of what drew me to *Lucinde*, and then ultimately to *Lucinda*, this attempt of mine to respond to Schlegel's writing. I found myself astonished that a book that seems so profoundly to anticipate the shape and concerns of much of the last century's writing could be so little attended to. But I really mean that Schlegel's book seemed to me, almost prophetically, to anticipate the shape and concerns of my own writing. Exactly prophetically, it turns out, judging by the contents of this present volume.

Schlegel's *Lucinde* sets out to demonstrate the possibility, or perhaps better the impossibility, of the correspondence of knowledge and its object, being a novella that contains its own theorization, or perhaps better fails to. *Lucinda*, in turn, is often engaged in looking after itself, maybe nowhere better or worse than in this very afterword. Neither case, though, should be mistaken for a purely intellectual problematic; in both, it seems to me, an essential and animating tension arises between the actuality of the author's lived situation and the attempt at representing that actuality, and simultaneously reflecting upon that representation.

The situation is complicated enough for Schlegel. In *Lucinda*, we have the further twist that part of the lived situation of its author is the sustained reading and engagement with Schlegel's earlier text. Often, that is to say, you may detect two or even three competing voices: that of the narrator of Schlegel's text, Julian, who survives rather more persistently than I originally expected him to; that of the reader/translator working through the linguistic, temporal, cultural, philosophical, and however many other boundaries that separate them from *Lucinde*; and that of the author (the author of the afterword, let's say) who occasionally uses this ongoing work as a springboard for engaging their own idiosyncratic concerns. The main structure of the piece arises out of this interplay, I think, though there are several other voices emerging here and there: the talking frog is Schlegel's, and the cast of *Friends* turn out (who would have expected it?) to take up many of the concerns of 1799's *Dialogue on Poetry*.

Two voices, perhaps, deserve special notice. Section 9 is devoted to guest spots by the poets Erín Moure and Minna Pam Dick. (At times I think of this section as akin to guest appearances on a hip hop record; other times, more like guest stars on a vintage sitcom. A little bit of both, I hope.) Both of these writers have been deeply inspiring to me in their explorations of the possibilities of translation once freed from the normative expectations of direct meaning transfer. Monica has more to say about Moure in section VII, and I would endorse almost all of that. I've written elsewhere about Dick's work. Suffice it to say that both of them in particular are acutely aware of the ways in which unsettling our expectations around translation can simultaneously open up novel ways of thinking about gender, politics, and identity; I find their work transfigurative in the largest sense.

The issue of translation is, to be sure, central to the project, as it has become increasingly central to my conception of poetry überhaupt. *Lucinda* is not, as I see it, a translation of Schlegel's novella, but it is founded upon an extended act of translation: one way I have found myself putting it is that translation might be considered the medium within which *Lucinda* is composed. That extended act of translation takes many forms: at times, the text approximates fairly closely a semantic translation of Schlegel's words, at times something more like paraphrase or summary, elsewhere the sound of Schlegel's German comes to the fore, or the associations sparked by the sounds and meanings found within *Lucinde*. And large swathes of the book, it must be said, are my own wayward interpolations. The intended effect, overall, is something like a visceral evocation of betweenness: between two languages, two eras, two histories of reading, two genres (it should not be forgotten that for Schlegel, the poetry of modernity was to be prose, even as the projected, never-written second half of *Lucinde* was to be a set of poems). It's this character of the book that renders the function of this little afterword one simply of orientation: there is no key to be given out, but I hope at least to have traced one or two avenues in.

Phillipe Lacoue-Labarthe and Jean-Luc Nancy, in their remarkable study of German Romanticism, *The Literary Absolute*, characterize the distinctively disorderly nature of Schlegel and his circle in these terms:

Romanticism, in other words, could never have protected, defended, or preserved itself from its "unworking"— its incalculable and uncontrollable incompletion: its incompletable incompletion. It could never, in other words, have avoided the most simple and derisory form of incompletion, the most accidental, as it were, or "empirical": that incompletion provoked by both character and circumstance (or persons and history), even though the exact degree of their respective agencies can never be known. In the case of Jena, they became quite jumbled: the fluctuations in intellectual moods and appetites, internal group rivalries, a certain laziness (or a virtuosity that came too easily), incertitude and the inability to dominate or "finish," permanent instability (outings, invitations, meetings, an impossible amount of activities), precipitation (and at times confusion), the overabundance of projects, the startling rapidity—all around them— of History itself, energy heedlessly wasted, death... Where, in the thousands of pages left behind by Jena... can anything be found that can be considered, without reservation, as a work?

There have been, in my own efforts, some decided reversals of this Schlegelian "unworking." Schlegel's own composition proceeded over the space of many months; *Lucinda* is the product of years, and years within which it acquired an almost alarmingly stable quality. Even if numerous other projects and concerns have popped up, it has been a centerpiece of my thinking and writing for quite some time. I am, of course, rather older than the earlier book's impetuous author. All the same, my fervent hope is to have preserved somewhere in this sometimes labyrinthine text a Schlegelian sense of incompletion, of a set of methods that in the end add up to no method at all. To the extent that this is a book with a politics, its concern is with opening a space for unpredictable and uncontrolled encounter, not a world remade but perhaps some first shoots, inklings. See what you think.

ACKNOWLEDGMENTS

An early version of section IV appeared in *The Arcadia Project*, ed. Joshua Corey and G. C. Waldrep (Ahsahta, 2012).

Sections I-IV can be found in the chapbook *Lucinda I-IV* (Spork, 2013).

Few of the jokes in section VI are original with me. Several are due to the late Henny Youngman. Others are due to the even later Sigmund Freud. The characters Rachel, Ross, Monica, Chandler, Joey, and Phoebe found in section VII are 18th century poets living in Jena, and for that reason cannot be identified with the characters of Rachel Green, Ross Geller, Monica Geller, Chandler Bing, Joey Tribbiani, and Phoebe Buffay, which are the property of Warner Bros. Entertainment, Inc. The subterranean section of section VII draws much of its vocabulary from *A Book Beginning What and Ending Away* by Clark Coolidge (Fence, 2013); *The Battlefield Where the Moon Says I Love You* by Frank Stanford (Lost Roads, 2000); and *Defoe* by Leslie Scalapino (O Books, 2002).

My source text for the composition throughout was the Studienausgabe edition of Friedrich Schlegel's *Lucinde* (Reclam, 1999).

Deepest thanks, once again, to Canarium: Nick, Robyn, Josh, and Lynn (& welcome, Issa!). & to guest artists Erín Moure and Minna Pam Dick. So many others have offered assistance or encouragement in one way or another that any attempt at a complete list would be impossible: I'll simply single out Joe Milutis for an enormously entertaining and instructive visit to Bothell, WA.

John Beer is the author of the poetry collections *The Waste Land and Other Poems* (2010), winner of the Norma Farber First Book Award from the Poetry Society of America, the chapbook *Lucinda* (2013), and the full-length *Lucinda* (2016). He lives in Portland, Oregon.